Suggestions

Set aside a regular time an[...] read
and pray undisturbed. Bef[...] u find
it helpful, use the BRF Pra[...]

In *Guidelines*, the introductory section provides context for the passages or themes to be studied, while the units of comment can be used daily, weekly or whatever best fits your timetable. You will need a Bible (more than one if you want to compare different translations) as Bible passages are not included. At the end of each week is a 'Guidelines' section, offering further thoughts about or practical application of what you have been studying.

Occasionally, you may read something in *Guidelines* that you find particularly challenging, even uncomfortable. This is inevitable in a series of notes which draws on a wide spectrum of contributors and doesn't believe in ducking difficult issues. Indeed, we believe that *Guidelines* readers much prefer thought-provoking material to a bland diet that only confirms what they already think.

If you do disagree with a contributor, you may find it helpful to go through these three steps. First, think about why you feel uncomfortable. Perhaps this is an idea that is new to you, or you are not happy about the way something has been expressed. Or there may be something more substantial – you may feel that the writer is guilty of sweeping generalisation, factual error, or theological or ethical misjudgement. Second, pray that God would use this disagreement to teach you more about his word and about yourself. Third, think about what you will do as a result of the disagreement. You might resolve to find out more about the issue, or write to the contributor or the editor of *Guidelines*.

To send feedback, please email **enquiries@brf.org.uk**, phone **+44 (0)1865 319700** or write to the address shown opposite.

Writers in this issue

George M. Wieland is the Director of Mission Research and Training at Carey Baptist College and Carey Graduate School, New Zealand. His background includes mission in Brazil, pastoring Baptist churches in the UK and teaching the New Testament. He is the author of *The Significance of Salvation* (Paternoster, 2006) and other publications on the Bible and mission.

David Dewey is a Baptist minister now serving both Baptist and Anglican communities in South Yorkshire. Alongside helping people engage with scripture, his interests include Bible translation and interpretation.

Kate Bruce is an RAF chaplain. In her previous role as Deputy Warden at Cranmer Hall, Durham, she taught preaching at BA and MA level. She did her PhD on preaching and imagination and now continues her work in teaching and researching on preaching, alongside her commitment to the RAF.

C.L. Crouch is David Allan Hubbard Professor of Old Testament at Fuller Theological Seminary and author of several books and numerous articles, including *An Introduction to the Study of Jeremiah* (Bloomsbury, 2017). She has particular interests in Old Testament ethics and in the prophetic books.

Andrew Francis is a URC minister, published poet/writer and community theologian. He is a popular conference speaker, congregational educator and Sunday preacher. His latest book is *Eat, Pray, Tell* (BRF, 2018).

Steve Walton is a researcher and teacher of the New Testament who serves as an Associate Research Fellow of Trinity College, Bristol. He is an Anglican priest, and has served in different ministries and taught in many colleges and universities. Steve is presently working on a major commentary on Acts.

Neil Le Tissier is a Regional Minister with the Heart of England Baptist Association, having previously served as Minister of Southborough Lane, and then Sutton Coldfield Baptist Churches. He contributed to *The NIV Comprehensive Concordance* (Hodder & Stoughton, 2001).

Henry Wansbrough OSB is a monk at Ampleforth Abbey in Yorkshire. He has been Chairman of the Oxford Faculty of Theology and a member of the Pope's Biblical Commission. More recently, he has been Professor of Biblical Studies at Liverpool Hope University. He has just published a new annotated version of the Bible, The Revised New Jerusalem Bible.

Conrad Gempf has been a Lecturer in New Testament at London School of Theology for more than 25 years. He is the author of several books on New Testament subjects, including *How to Like Paul Again* (Authentic, 2013).

David Spriggs writes...

The next four months have as their spiritual focus the celebration of the Feast of Pentecost, when we commemorate again the gift of the Holy Spirit to the gathered disciples, with all the implications for communicating the gospel, the empowering for mission and the reproduction in our lives of the character of Jesus.

This issue of *Guidelines* engages with several of these great themes. Kate Bruce offers us some reflections on the role of the Holy Spirit in communicating. David Dewey also offers us different ways of reading the Bible which are themselves formed by approaches found within scripture.

George M. Wieland takes us through Acts, looking at it through a mission and spirituality lens. By drawing on his own cross-cultural experience and linking it with his passion for mission, he brings fresh insight and challenges to this foundational text for the church's mission today.

If Acts is the foundational text, then Romans could claim to be the foundational epistle. Conrad Gempf gives us a short overview of this great letter – but with a twist. He draws attention to how one chapter's teaching should influence our understanding of another chapter. This makes for a fascinating rereading of Romans.

In the description of the fruit of the Spirit is peace. Andrew Francis, a new writer for *Guidelines*, focuses on shalom, bringing to us his insights through the text of both the Old and New Testaments.

In addition to all of these, we have substantial contributions from Steve Walton, who continues taking us through the second half of Luke's gospel, and also from C.L. Crouch on that fascinating and heart-searching prophetic book of Hosea. Neil le Tissier helps us appreciate the significance of metaphors as a form of divine and human communication by unpacking 'trees' in the Bible. And Father Henry Wansbrough uses his extensive biblical knowledge to examine some of the key passages in 1 Chronicles.

Finally, I have some exciting news: Dr Helen Paynter will take over as commissioning editor in the September–December 2019 issue. Helen left a career in hospital medicine in 2008 to obey the call to Baptist ministry. She trained at Bristol Baptist College, and then went on to combine pastoral ministry at Victoria Park Baptist Church, Bristol, with further study, doing her doctorate in the Old Testament. She is now Director of the Centre for the Study of Bible and Violence at Bristol Baptist College, and Associate Minister of Westbury on Trym Baptist Church, Bristol.

My prayer is that, through all of these enriching notes, our awareness of the life-giving power of God's Holy Spirit will be increased.

The BRF Prayer

Almighty God,
you have taught us that your word is a lamp for our feet
and a light for our path. Help us, and all who prayerfully
read your word, to deepen our fellowship with you
and with each other through your love.
And in so doing may we come to know you more fully,
love you more truly, and follow more faithfully
in the steps of your son Jesus Christ, who lives and reigns
with you and the Holy Spirit, one God for evermore.
Amen

Acts: participating in the unfolding mission of God

George M. Wieland

In Luke's gospel, Jesus, anointed by the Spirit, announces and demonstrates the arrival of the long-awaited kingdom of God. A group of followers gathers around him. They begin to comprehend who he is and to learn a new way of living, relating and serving together under his leadership. In Luke's second volume, the book of Acts, those followers, empowered by the same Spirit, witness to the world that their risen, exalted Lord calls all to acknowledge him, trust in him and enter into the reality of shared life under his rule.

The narrative of Acts pulsates with movement. It unfolds geographically, from beginnings in Jerusalem through Judea, across into Samaria and around the Mediterranean world until the book reaches its conclusion with the proclamation of the kingdom of God in Rome, the capital city of the empire. Political, ethnic, social, religious and cultural boundaries are crossed as the radical nature of this kingdom comes into sharper profile in the context of mission. A remarkably diverse cast of characters comes into view, proclaiming, receiving or resisting the new kingdom. Diverse, countercultural communities emerge in which the risen Jesus is active and kingdom life is shared.

Old disputes over whether the book of Acts should be regarded as history or theology are now seen to be outmoded. The writing of history always involves interpretation and an account may be written in such a way as to draw out theological significance while still being true to what actually took place. Acts may be read as a narrative of real people and events through which the activity of God's Spirit is discerned and God's mission is realised. Furthermore, since that mission continues today in our own contexts, we should expect resonances between the story recorded in Acts and the continuing story in which we participate.

Unless otherwise stated, scripture quotations are from the New Revised Standard Version (Anglicised).

1 Give up your own agenda

Acts 1:1–14

In the opening paragraphs of Acts, we meet people who were to be leaders in the church's mission. There was a major obstacle, however, to their effectiveness in that role. Even after the risen Jesus had spent 40 days with them, 'speaking about the kingdom of God' (v. 3), their vision of that kingdom was far too small. 'Lord,' they asked, 'is this the time when you will restore the kingdom to Israel?' (v. 6). In their minds, this kingdom was surely their kingdom, for their people, in their place, with a king ruling in their city and no doubt significant positions for his friends. Their best hope for the future was a restoration of their nation to the glories of a past age.

Jesus' reply (vv. 7–8) pointed them to a new way of looking for the kingdom that went far beyond those expectations. It was to be not only in their place but in every place; not only for their people but for all peoples; realised not through the acquisition of political power but by the empowering of God's Spirit for witness to Jesus, risen and reigning. This constituted a challenge to surrender their own agendas and have their horizons of what God was intending to do stretched beyond their own immediate interests and concerns. It also shifted the question from what Jesus would now do for them to what they were to be and to do as his servants and as participants in his mission.

Even with that reorientation, do we detect some reluctance on the part of the apostles to move on from the place where they had witnessed the ascension of Jesus, as there had been at the transfiguration (vv. 9–11; compare Luke 9:28–36)? That's understandable. The mountain was a place of peace, remote from the everyday world, where they had been enjoying the company of the risen Jesus, having their hearts stirred as he spoke of the kingdom of God. The city, by contrast, was a place of challenge and vulnerability. It would have been easier to wait on the mountain for the promised power, and then venture more confidently into the hard place. But the promise to them, and to successive participants in God's mission, is of enabling at the point and in the place where it is needed. Mission requires going vulnerably into that place, and waiting there for the Spirit to enable and help.

2 To all the world, through all God's people

Acts 2:1–21

When it did come, the empowering that the disciples received was utterly different to anything they might have envisaged. There, in the city and at the right time, the Spirit enabled them to communicate the reality of God and his saving power, with the result that the ears and hearts of thousands were opened to the good news about Jesus. And who were those thousands? Luke emphasises the presence in Jerusalem of 'devout Jews from every nation under heaven' (v. 5). They were diaspora people from the Jewish communities scattered around the Mediterranean and beyond. On that significant day when the Spirit of God was poured out in a dramatic manifestation of the presence and glory of God, it was people of the diaspora who felt the impact. The Pentecost miracle meant that they not only heard with their ears but also knew in their hearts that what had happened in Jerusalem in the raising up of Jesus as Lord and Messiah (2:36) was of urgent relevance not only to them but also to their places and peoples.

There are more diaspora people in the world today than ever before. According to United Nations statistics, there are currently 244 million people who have moved from their countries of birth to live elsewhere. Migration and migrants have always had a vital role in the mission of God. The experience of dislocation often results in greater openness to new learning and, indeed, to God. Once the gospel has become known, the transnational networks of migrants become avenues along which it can spread. An urgent task for the church in migrant-receiving countries and other contexts of increasing diversity is to learn how to relate and communicate across linguistic and cultural barriers so that dislocated people may find a place of belonging with them in God's kingdom.

A remarkable feature of Pentecost was the participation of the whole community of believers in this witness to the nations. Peter recognised the fulfilment of God's promise to pour out the Spirit not only on a handful of key leaders but on 'all flesh', women and men, young and old, slaves and free (vv. 17–18, quoting Joel 2:28–29). Where churches understand ministry as the activity of a few overworked professionals, and formally or informally restrict access to those roles on grounds of gender, age or socio-economic status, Pentecost continues to present both an uncomfortable challenge and an exhilarating promise.

3 Sharing life in the kingdom community

Acts 2:37–47; 4:32–37

Coming under the lordship of Jesus and entering into life in the Spirit brought the believers into community with each other. And what a community! They were always found together, at the temple and in homes, worshipping, praying, learning eagerly from those who had been with Jesus, experiencing God's power in remarkable ways. They also enjoyed the mundane but no less remarkable miracle of enough to eat every day. This happened as those who had food shared it generously and those with material wealth offered it to meet the needs of those without. Little wonder that their witness to the risen Jesus was powerfully effective (4:33) and many were drawn to join them (2:47).

That principle of living generously so that no one in the community would be in need was part of the blueprint for the communal life of Israel set out in the book of Deuteronomy. The promise that there would be 'no one in need among you' (Deuteronomy 15:4, echoed in Acts 4:34) becomes a reality as those who have resources open their hearts and hands to those around them who are in need (Deuteronomy 15:7–11). Luke is indicating that where Jesus rules, God's intention for flourishing community is realised.

There were in Israel groups that went beyond acts of generosity to renouncing personal ownership of their possessions and embracing a communal economic life. These were the Essene communities that, according to the Jewish writer Philo, were found in many of the towns and villages of Judea. They functioned socially and economically as kinship groups, substitute families for those who became members. Like monastic communities in later Christian traditions, they maintained houses of hospitality for the poor, the sick, lepers or travellers. It is possible that it was an Essene hospitality house in Bethany ('Beth-anya', possibly 'house of the poor') that Jesus and his disciples stayed in as pilgrims from Galilee to the Jerusalem festivals.

Whatever specific form it might have taken, the shared life of the Jerusalem church went far deeper than is suggested by the English term 'fellowship' (2:42). In the privatised cultures of much of the western world, it might seem adequate to chat over coffee after a Sunday service before plunging back into individual lives largely disconnected from those they refer to as their family in Christ. The arrival of refugees and other migrants shaped by communal cultures, however, might catalyse a rediscovery of more authentic community and kinship.

4 Prayer in alignment with the mission of God

Acts 4:13–31

Prayer percolates through the narrative of Acts. It is the constant activity of the groups of disciples as they wait in Jerusalem between the ascension of Jesus and Pentecost (1:14); it is through prayer that this group commits to God the choice of an apostle to replace Judas (1:24–25); prayer characterises the daily life of the Pentecost community (2:42); they continue to participate in the regular temple prayers (3:1); it is a ministry priority for the apostles (6:4); with prayer people are commissioned for ministry (6:6); the last breath of Stephen the martyr is prayer, entrusting his spirit to Jesus and seeking forgiveness for his killers (7:59–60); and on through some 32 specific references. Prayer is intrinsic to the story of mission.

For all that, the actual content of the prayers is not reported, with the exception of Stephen's dying words (7:59–60) and this prayer of the church (vv. 24–30). The setting is the first recorded experience of official persecution. Peter and John had healed a beggar at the temple gate and proclaimed that this had been done in the power of Jesus, who had been raised from the dead and was now exercising divine authority (3:1–26). This had led to their arrest, imprisonment and appearance before the council. Hoping to put an end to this new movement before it spread any further, the leaders of the people had warned the apostles to stop what they were doing and specifically to speak no more in the name of Jesus.

At this crisis point for the Jesus community, their immediate recourse was to prayer. They affirmed who God is, the ruler and creator of all things; they found in scripture (Psalm 2) a framework within which to interpret the opposition that first Jesus himself and now they were experiencing; they held to what they had come to believe about Jesus and had experienced of God's Spirit; and they prayed, not for their own safety but for God to continue to act, for courage to play their part and for the name of Jesus to be vindicated.

In post-Christendom societies, where assumptions of the church's place in national life still linger, it can be difficult to comprehend the threat to the very existence of Christian communities that followers of Jesus face in many other contexts today. For them and for all of us, the response of that first Christian community models prayer in alignment with the saving mission of God.

5 From problems of difference to the potential of diversity

Acts 6:1–15

Cross-cultural mission generates multicultural community. The Pentecost miracle had brought into being a diverse body of people. There were the Galilean followers of Jesus and others from Jerusalem and the regions round about. They would have been among the 'Hebrews' that Luke mentions (v. 1). The Pentecost miracle had then added a large number of diaspora Jews who were in Jerusalem at that time. Some would have travelled to worship at the festivals; others might have relocated permanently to Jerusalem. Luke calls them 'Hellenists' (v. 1): not Greeks but Jews exhibiting aspects of the Greek cultures of their places of origin and probably using Greek as their main language of communication.

It was not long before this new community, trying to function as a kinship group for purposes of mutual support, was experiencing tensions. But the strains exposed a cultural fault line. The diaspora 'outsiders' had the impression that the local 'insiders' were getting preferential treatment. It came down to access to resources, which involved having the connections with the people responsible for them; locals tend to have such connections, while immigrants do not.

It began as grumbling. Wisely, the apostles didn't get defensive. They acknowledged the problem and offered a pathway forward. New appointments were made to the community's leadership. But look at those names (v. 5) – all seven are Greek. Those appointed came from the 'outsiders' group that was feeling discriminated against and wondering if they really belonged with the local 'insiders'.

Tracking the Acts narrative, this episode precipitates a dramatic reorientation outwards. Those Hellenistic believers appointed to community leadership roles did much more than 'wait at tables' (v. 2). Stephen, now validated by recognition within the community, reached out boldly to other diaspora Jews. This provoked a violent backlash (vv. 8–15), but out of his martyrdom came both increased persecution and exponential growth. It was Philip, not the original apostles who had heard Jesus' commission to go beyond Jerusalem (1:8), who crossed the boundary separating Jews from Samaritans to take the gospel to Samaria (8:4–25).

The grumbling was not only silenced; it was turned into growth. And that continues to happen when 'outsiders' who have natural openings into a wider world join the church's leadership and, with the church's backing, extend the scope of its mission far beyond the imagination of the 'insiders'. There is enormous potential for the church's health and mission in recognising and affirming gifted people from outside traditional leadership groups.

6 Who's passing through?

Acts 8:26–40

So far in the mission narrative of Acts, we have seen crowds impacted with the witness to and demonstration of the kingly authority of Jesus. The next three chapters, however, relate how God dealt with individual people to bring revelation of and commitment to Jesus. In each case, human agents are impelled by divine communication to travel to specific places to encounter particular people in whom God is already at work. Mission often seems to take the form of God bringing people who are seeking him into engagement with people whom he is preparing to act as his messengers.

In today's passage, Philip, one of the seven Hellenists appointed to serve the Jerusalem church and subsequently the pioneer of mission to Samaria, is prompted by an angel to travel to a desert road. There, he receives further prompting from God to enter into conversation with a distinguished traveller, the royal treasurer of the Candace, queen of Ethiopia. Luke does not make clear the precise relationship of this man to Judaism, whether he was a diaspora Jew or a Gentile God-worshipper. It is also uncertain whether the term 'eunuch' necessarily represents a castrated male; it could refer to a court official more generally. It could well be, however, that the appearance of this traveller in the unfolding story of mission points to the extension of the witness to Christ in two ways. The witness is carried to 'the ends of the earth' (1:8), which for some ancient writers was represented by Ethiopia. It also includes people, such as eunuchs and foreigners, who had been marginalised and excluded from full participation in the worship of the people of God (compare Isaiah 56:3–8).

Philip's part in this story repays reflection, with his attentiveness to God's prompting, his obedience, courage and willingness to (literally) journey alongside the seeker, and the dialogical and responsive mode of his engagement. The place of the encounter is also significant. The witness of a community of believers in a settled location can be very effective, as it had been in Jerusalem (2:43–47). There, the church's shared life as well as its words had impacted those who lived in proximity to them. The story of this Ethiopian traveller alerts us to the potential of encounters on the road for revelation and transformation. Who is passing through? And what might be the questions that are occupying them on their journey?

Guidelines

- What is your understanding of the scope of the kingdom of God? What does it mean for you to seek it?

- Does your ministry and mission agenda align with that which Jesus articulates in 1:7–8?

- Do the diaspora people in your neighbourhood know that the God whom local Christians worship also cares about them? Do they ever hear about this God in their native/heart languages?

- Are there people in your own church or mission context of whom little is expected because of their gender, age or socio-economic or other status? Consider the potential if their participation were empowered.

- What could the economic dimension of life as a kingdom community look like in the context of your local church? If realised, what would be different about its worship, discipleship and mission?

- Consider a particular challenge facing the Christian community in a local, national or international context that you know. Using 4:24–30 as a template, compose a prayer bringing that situation before God and seeking alignment with the mission of God in it.

- Do issues in your faith community reveal inequities between more- and less-privileged groups? If so, how might those be addressed?

- Does the leadership team of your church or Christian organisation reflect the diversity of the community it serves? How might able people from under-represented groups be identified and validated in ministry?

- When did you last follow the prompting of the Spirit to go to a surprising place?

- What may be learned about a mission approach from Philip's engagement with the Ethiopian eunuch?

1 'Brother Saul'

Acts 9:1–31

A 'road to Damascus' experience has entered the English lexicon to refer to a dramatic change in attitude and direction brought about by a sudden insight. It is possible, however, to overstate how instantaneous the change in Saul was, and to overlook other factors that contributed to his transformation from persecutor of the church to proclaimer of the faith (Galatians 1:23).

When official opposition to the Jesus movement was gathering momentum, there was a telling intervention by a respected Pharisee and council member named Gamaliel. With the mood of the council turning towards ordering the execution of the apostles, Gamaliel advised caution. 'If this plan or this undertaking is of human origin,' he argued, 'it will fail; but if it is of God, you will not be able to overthrow them – in that case you may even be found fighting against God!' (5:33–39). Gamaliel was Saul's teacher (22:3). As the young man relentlessly pursued those who professed allegiance to Jesus, did his teacher's warning niggle in his mind?

Saul first enters the Acts narrative as an observer at the lynching of the first Christian martyr (7:54—8:1). Stephen's challenging witness to Jesus as the righteous one whom God had raised up as prophet and ruler had so inflamed the council that they apparently abandoned due process and took the law into their own hands. Saul was there, approving, guarding the coats of those who stoned him to death. But he saw Stephen's Spirit-filled adoration of his Lord and heard his testimony to the exalted Jesus and his prayer of forgiveness for his murderers. Did this prepare Saul to hear from heaven the one whom Stephen professed to see there?

And there was Ananias, devout, law-observant, respected within the Jewish community in Damascus (22:12). He was a believer in Jesus, and it was Jesus himself who charged him with the terrifying mission of seeking out his persecutor, praying for his healing and embracing him into the community that he had set out to destroy (vv. 10–18). Was 'brother' the first word that Saul heard from a follower of Jesus after his encounter with the risen Lord?

Gamaliel offering godly wisdom; Stephen uttering Spirit-enabled testimony; Ananias extending Christ-like grace – none of them could have comprehended exactly how they were participating in a process of grace that Paul was later to affirm had begun in him in his mother's womb (Galatians 1:15).

2 Discomfort

Acts 10:1–23

The dramatic encounter between the apostle Peter and his companions and the household of the Gentile army officer Cornelius is of such significance for Luke that, as with the meeting of Saul with the exalted Jesus on the road to Damascus (9:1–19a; 22:6–16; 26:12–18), he includes it three times. A full account is given in the third person (10:1–48), then Peter provides a first-person account (11:1–18), and it features again in Peter's decisive intervention in the deliberations of the Jerusalem Council (15:7–11, 14). Evidently, for Luke the historian-theologian, these two incidents are central to his narrative and its message. One relates the calling of the apostle to the Gentiles. The other describes the saving of a Gentile household. Both involve the reorientation of key participants towards the goal and character of God's mission to the nations.

While it might be natural for Christian readers to identify with and focus on Peter the missionary, this episode begins with Cornelius. The one to whom Peter would be sent was already a worshipper of God, eager to know and serve God. It was Peter who had to be 'converted' if he was to be a participant in what God was doing. This process involved intense discomfort. Perhaps he had already moved some way towards the margins of religious acceptability by accepting hospitality in the home-workshop of a tanner, but the vision that he received startled and challenged him to go beyond anything he could have imagined. While he waited for dinner on the flat roof, the smells of the tannery wafted around him and the sun beat down on a tarpaulin that provided some shade. Suddenly, the scene morphed into a sheet lowered from heaven bearing all manner of living creatures, which he was invited to take as food. To his horrified objection, on grounds of dietary and religious purity, he received the reply, 'What God has made clean, you must not call profane' (v. 15).

Of course, this profoundly disorientating experience had implications for how Peter should regard not only food but also people whom he had placed in the category of religiously unclean and unacceptable to God. As his prejudice began to be broken down, three people in that 'unclean' category arrived at the house. It took direct reassurance by the Spirit to persuade Peter to act in accordance with this developing reorientation, and welcome them in.

3   Discovery

Acts 10:23–48

The concept of liminality (from Latin *limen*, 'threshold') was utilised by anthropologist Victor Turner and others to denote that in-between state experienced when one settled mode of existence has been left behind and what will be the new settled state has not yet been entered into. Liminality is a space of disruption, loss, uncertainty, anxiety; but it is also pregnant with new possibilities. Peter and his companions were already experiencing such liminality as they struggled to make sense of the disorientating journey, both outer and inner, that they had embarked upon. Now, they were to enter a literal liminal space as they crossed the threshold into a Gentile home.

Peter's discomfort is visceral. First, as is often the case in initial cross-cultural encounters, there had been a painfully awkward moment. In his overeagerness to welcome and show respect to God's messenger, Cornelius had prostrated himself before him in worship (v. 25). 'Stand up,' Peter protested, 'I am only a mortal' (v. 26). Once inside, his discomfort and inner tension show through in his need to make clear to this unprecedented audience of a Gentile household that 'you yourselves know that it is unlawful for a Jew to associate with or to visit a Gentile' (v. 28).

Discomfort precedes discovery. As Peter heard Cornelius' testimony of his experience with God and saw that home crowded with Gentiles eager to hear whatever message God had for them, something happened. 'I truly understand that God shows no partiality' (v. 34), Peter's words, could be read as the statement of a settled conviction explaining why he had made the decision to take the gospel to Gentiles. The Greek verb *katalambanomai*, however, is in the present tense, and is better understood as an exclamation of a dawning realisation: 'I'm really getting it!' (The NIV translation tries to capture this sense with 'I now realise…') It is as he steps out in obedience, despite his discomfort, that Peter is able to grasp more fully the scope and character of the mission of God.

From the day of Pentecost onwards, Peter had been proclaiming that Jesus is Lord of all, and that all who believe in Jesus receive forgiveness of sins. Now, however, the presence and activity of God in that Gentile home, evidenced by the outpouring of the Holy Spirit, persuaded Peter that the 'all' whom God was eager to accept extended beyond those with whom he shared a geographical, cultural or religious identity.

4 Grace seen

Acts 11:19–26

The establishing of the first genuinely interethnic Jesus community, in the Syrian city of Antioch, is of incalculable significance for the mission story of Acts and indeed for the history of Christianity. This was to be the church that commissioned Barnabas and Saul for the work of mission that occupies much of the remainder of the book.

It is not always noticed that those whose witness and courageous boundary-crossing pioneered this remarkable Jesus community were refugees. Taking the gospel to Antioch had not been the result of a strategic plan nor a well-resourced mission enterprise. It was people scattered by the persecution in Jerusalem who had made their way up the coast to another country, where they would have arrived like all refugees, suffering trauma and loss, without resources or a right to belong, hoping to find some place of safety and means of survival. Yet these 'scattered' people (Greek *diaspeirō*, v. 19; compare 8:4) were at the same time a 'sowing' people (Greek *speirō*; see Luke 8:5). Their witness to Jesus and the message of the kingdom went with them.

The great breakthrough in Antioch happened when some of these scattered believers looked beyond people like themselves and shared the good news with people of a different ethnicity and culture. Most of the believers related only to people like themselves (v. 19), but there were some who had the capacity and the courage to reach beyond their own group (v. 20). It is no accident that these were bicultural people, diaspora Jews (from that same term, *diaspeirō*) originally from Cyprus and the North African region of Cyrene. They inhabited both the Jewish world and the Roman world, but were on the margins of each. Perhaps it is those who live on the margins who are best able to cross boundaries.

When the Jerusalem church heard reports of non-Jews being brought into the community, there may have been concerns. Barnabas was sent to investigate. He 'saw the grace of God' and rejoiced (v. 23). As Luke glosses, it took 'a good man, full of the Holy Spirit and of faith' (v. 24) to see beyond past experience of God and the church to discern God's grace operative in fresh ways. It was also Barnabas who was able to see beyond what Saul had been to envisage what, by God's grace, he would become, and open a door for him to exercise the ministry to which God had called him (vv. 25–26).

5 Grace extended

Acts 11:27–30; 12:25—13:12

The Antioch church, built by bicultural people who could reach beyond people like themselves, nurtured by pastors who could recognise and rejoice in the surprising grace of God, was a church that soon learnt to respond to the needs of others. They were evidently not only open to God within their own fellowship, but also receptive to the ministry that came to them from other churches. It was through a prophet from Jerusalem that God let them know that a severe famine was ahead, bringing insufferable hardship for the remnants of the persecuted church in Judea. Their response was to determine to give. This church, born in a refugee community, understood hardship, and they responded with empathy and generosity. The first mission from the Antioch church was to take financial help to brothers and sisters in Christ who were in desperate need elsewhere (11:27–30).

The work of mission had been very fruitful in Antioch. The church had grown in numbers, was being built up in faith and understanding, was open to God's voice and was living in loving relationship with other believers. A foundational role in all this had been played by the pastor-teachers, Barnabas and Saul (11:26). But along with the Cypriot Jew Barnabas and Saul, the rabbi from Tarsus, there were others: Simeon, whom they called Niger ('Black'), an African; Lucius, who might have been among those

Cyrenians (from North Africa) who broke through to reach non-Jews with the gospel; and Manaen, probably of a noble Jewish family connected with the Herodian dynasty. They not only ministered together but also practised spiritual disciplines of worship and fasting together. And it was this diverse, multicultural ministry team that was able to hear the Holy Spirit's prompting to look beyond themselves, their own ministries and the church in which they had invested so much, and to embrace the call to a wider participation in God's mission to the world.

The cost to the Antioch church must have been immense. But the grace that Barnabas had discerned at work in them from the beginning was now extended through them to other regions and peoples. In commissioning their valued ministers and friends Barnabas and Saul (13:3), this mission community was so attuned to God's heart and purpose that the sending by the church was at the same time a sending by the Holy Spirit (13:4).

6 Resources for transformation

Acts 15:1–35

Reaching out generates issues of receiving in. As the mission narrative of Acts has progressed, an increasingly diverse collection of people have been finding themselves in relationship with each other through their shared allegiance to Jesus Christ as Lord. This has raised important issues. Who may be received into the Jesus-worshipping community, and what is asked of them in order for that to happen? And what changes in attitude, practice and even belief are required of the church so that it is able not only to include those who had previously been outside the group but also to embrace a new, more diverse identity? Acts 15 describes a process of communal discernment that enabled key changes to be named and a new identity owned. It opened the door for Gentiles to be welcomed into the Jesus movement and brought the church to understand itself as an ethnically and culturally diverse community of people who acknowledged each other to be equally loved, called and accepted by God.

That process drew on several resources. There were stories from the edge of missional engagement, as Paul and Barnabas shared things they had encountered beyond the existing church that they were convinced were God's doing (vv. 3–4, 12). There were questions from the centre, as the holders of the traditions of the community that had come into being in Jerusalem highlighted issues that those new ways posed for what they had previously thought and practised (v. 5). There was personal testimony, as the respected and trusted leader Simon Peter told of how God had dealt with him to challenge his assumptions about God and others, and to reveal God's heart for people whom he had considered outside the scope of God's acceptance (vv. 7–9). There was wise leadership, giving space for all those voices, articulating what was being discerned as the direction in which God was leading, and offering a pathway forward (vv. 13–21). And, crucial for the community's recognition of God's purpose in those strange new circumstances, there was scripture. Rereading the text in the light of those experiences and issues, aspects they might not have noticed before were thrown into sharper profile (vv. 15–17; compare Amos 9:11–12) and its significance for their time and its challenges were unleashed. Through all of that they came to have confidence that the Holy Spirit was leading them together in the direction of God's purpose and mission (v. 28).

Guidelines

- Reflect on the work of God in your life. Who are some of the people who have participated in it?

- What opportunities do you have to contribute godly wisdom, costly testimony or gracious acceptance to other people's journeys of faith, growth and service?

- When did you last feel challenged by God to change your attitude to other cultures or behaviours?

- How are you going to act on a changed or changing attitude to a person or group?

- Find – and take – an opportunity to enter what for you will be liminal space. What are you discovering there?

- Reflect on the key truths about Jesus that Peter shared in 10:34–43.

- Are there people whom you find yourself reluctant to welcome into your church community? What would it take to change your mind?

- Consider some new or experimental expression of church or mission. Can you see the grace of God in it? How do you recognise it?

- Is there someone whom others struggle to accept because of their past life for whom you could open doors into the service to which God has called them?

- Read or listen to reports of hunger or other tangible need beyond your own immediate community. Consider the response that you could make, according to your ability.

- If you are involved in church or other leadership, how would you be able to hear if God were requiring you or a colleague to serve elsewhere?

- Identify an issue currently presenting challenges for your Christian community. Consider how the resources utilised by the Jerusalem Council might be drawn upon in a process of communal discernment. How are voices from the edge going to be heard; questions from the centre welcomed; personal testimony respected; scripture reread in relation to that issue?

1 When doors close

Acts 15:36—16:10

Acts 16:9–10 is sometimes cited as a paradigmatic story of God's guidance in mission. Certainly, Paul's vision of the Macedonian appealing for help had the effect of stretching the mission horizon and bringing clear direction. The full story of God's leading, however, can be traced back to the beginning of this episode in 15:36. There is no mention there of any special sign, simply a good idea: something like 'Let's go and visit the new believers and see how they're doing.' It was no light matter to consider returning to the scenes of hostility, misunderstanding and violence that they had experienced in those locations (chapters 13—14). Paul's proposal was evidence of an attitude of selfless concern for those who had become believers. Sometimes, that is all the guidance that is needed.

The two leaders, however, found that they were unable to agree on the composition of their mission team (15:37–40). Perhaps Barnabas, the persistent encourager, wanted to reinstate John Mark after earlier disappointment (13:13), whereas Paul felt that mission required proven participants.

Ultimately, tempers flared ('sharp disagreement' doesn't quite do justice to the colourful Greek term *paroxysmos* in 15:39). Was this disruption in relationship going to derail the mission? In the event, each continued to serve, but, for now, they served separately. And the personal notes in Paul's letters show that at some point relationships were restored (Colossians 4:10; 2 Timothy 4:11).

There were further obstacles. The Roman province of Asia (roughly present-day Turkey) appeared to be a strategic mission destination, but the missionaries were 'forbidden by the Holy Spirit to speak the word' there (16:6). In fact, chapters 19—20 describe the spectacularly effective mission that Paul exercised later in Asia's main city, Ephesus. Perhaps the Spirit's 'No' was, in this instance, a 'Not yet'. The team then set its sights on the north-eastern province of Bithynia, but again the Spirit did not allow them (16:7). As far as we know, Paul never did reach Bithynia, but it is listed among the communities addressed in 1 Peter 1:1. Perhaps this 'No' was a 'Not you'.

Finally, when they were literally at the end of the road, the sign was given (16:9–10). But it still had to be interpreted, in community (now including Luke, as indicated by the shift from 'they' to 'we') and within the framework of their understanding of God's purpose of salvation for the world and their call to participate in it.

2 Households in mission

Acts 16:11–40

The shift of scene in this episode represents new challenges for the mission group. They are now in the province of Macedonia and in Philippi, which took pride in being a 'leading city' (v. 12) of the region. Since it was neither the capital nor the largest city, this designation probably reflects its status as a *kolōnia* of Rome. Paul's usual practice as he travelled was to join the Jewish community in the synagogue, where, as a visiting rabbi, he might be invited to bring a message (13:5, 14; 14:1; 17:1–3, 10, 17; 18:4; 19:8). In Philippi, however, Paul and the others went looking for a 'place of prayer' (v. 13) outside the city. Possibly the Jewish community in that city could not muster the requisite ten males to form a synagogue, but there was a group of women who met to pray, at least one of whom was very receptive to their message.

Thyatira, in Roman Asia, was the source of dye used to manufacture the expensive purple cloth that was restricted to people of high status and wealth. Dealers in purple cloth could themselves become quite wealthy, though it's possible that Lydia was a freedwoman (former slave) who continued to work in her master's business. In any event, the absence of any reference to a husband or other *paterfamilias* (male household head) suggests that she herself was the head of the household, probably comprising slaves or other employees in addition to Lydia, into which she invited the missionaries (v. 15). This was more than the provision of accommodation. Lydia's household became the relational nucleus of a new community of believers (v. 40). She was the 'person of peace' for Philippi (compare Luke 10:5–7).

A second household comes into view. Beaten and imprisoned after Paul had released a female slave from spirit-possession, with economic consequences for her owners, Paul and Silas refused to profit from a sudden earthquake that created opportunity for escape. The officer in charge could well have been a retired centurion, settled in the colony after his military service, where he could at last establish a home and raise a family. He and his entire household responded to the missionaries' message and were baptised.

A woman, a slave and a Gentile. Mission in this Roman colony demonstrates the nature of another kind of kingdom, open to all without distinction of gender, social status or ethnicity.

3 Common ground and holy ground

Acts 17:16–34

Visitors to Athens today are still awed by the distinctive Acropolis, the immense temples and the larger-than-life statues. Those sights greeted Paul on his arrival. Athens was not actually in the strategic mission plan! The situation in Macedonia had become threatening, and the new believers had hurried Paul away and sent him off by ship. Friends got him as far as Athens, where he was to wait until the rest of his team joined him. What ensued, however, was not an uneventful few days of rest and recuperation. The unplanned stopover yielded an astonishing example of cross-cultural, contextual mission engagement, demonstrating dispositions, practices and a theological perspective that are exemplary for mission in any place and at any time.

Paul looked (vv. 16, 22–23), but not merely to take in the sights. He 'looked carefully' at the shrines, temples and idols (v. 23), making an effort to understand the people of that place and what and whom they worshipped. He opened himself to be emotionally engaged by what he saw (v. 16), responding with a deeply felt concern for the honour of the one true God and compassion for those whose hopes, prayers and religious activity were futile. And his stance was positive. In all that activity, he was willing to recognise an earnest quest for God (vv. 22–23).

He listened. Paul's address to the Areopagus, the council that governed the religious life of the city, displays a thorough knowledge of the Stoic philosophy that framed the worldview of many in the Greek world in terms of human origins and divine rule (vv. 24–27). He also, astonishingly, cites affirmations about the deity that might be heard in pagan worship addressed to Zeus (v. 28). He travelled as far as possible on common ground before introducing the distinctive difference in his Christian witness (vv. 30–31).

This reveals the theological perspective out of which Paul travelled, engaged, suffered and hoped. He ventured into the world confident that, wherever he went, God was already there. Each place had been created by God, and its people were there by God's purpose. It was God's intention that in that place those people might yearn for and reach out to God. Mission was not taking God into a place from which God had been absent and to people who were far from God. It consisted of opening people's eyes to the God who was there, and not far from any of them. The common ground was indeed holy ground.

4 'I have many people in this city'

Acts 18

Whereas much of the activity in the gospels takes place in towns and villages, hillsides and seashores, the mission story of Acts is predominantly urban. It therefore resonates increasingly in this 'urban century', in which for the first time in human history a majority of the world's population lives in cities. Of course, the size and scale of today's cities are far greater than those of the cities where the first Jesus communities lived out their new faith, but there are certain urban features experienced across time. Cities typically have diverse populations, ethnically and socially, with relatively high degrees of mobility. They are destinations for the poor and the uprooted, for seekers of opportunity or anonymity. They require administrative, economic and service infrastructures. They exist in dynamic relationship with both their rural hinterlands and with national and transnational political, economic and cultural forces. They are centres of manufacturing and trade, of education and popular entertainment. Then, as now, cities presented both daunting challenges and stunning opportunities for mission.

The narrative of Paul's 18-month stay in Corinth is richly peopled with urban characters. There is the Jewish couple, Priscilla and Aquila, on the move because of political hostility in Rome (vv. 1–4, 18, 26). It might have been economic opportunity that drew them to Corinth, as the Isthmian Games, temporarily swelling the city's population, meant business opportunities for tent-makers. There were leaders of the strong Jewish community in Corinth, such as Crispus and his household (v. 8) and Sosthenes (v. 17). There is the Roman Titius Justus, who, as a Gentile God-fearer, had joined with the worship of the synagogue next door to his house (v. 7). There is the proconsul Gallio, enjoying a notable political career comparable to that of his better-known younger brother, Seneca (vv. 12–17). From the dates of Gallio's proconsulship, we can place Paul's stay in Corinth at around AD50–52.

Urban mission practitioners know the sense of being overwhelmed by the scale and complexity of their urban contexts, by teeming, diverse populations, by the pressures of political, economic and social forces. They can feel vulnerable, impotent, isolated. This seems to have been Paul's experience. It took a gracious divine intervention in the form of a vision to reassure him that, although to his eyes that great population might have seemed unknowable, the Lord saw it differently: 'I have many people in this city' (v. 10, NIV).

5 Who am I? And for what?

Acts 21:37—22:29

'Saul of Tarsus' identifies Paul as a native of a notable Mediterranean port and centre of Greek learning at the south-western corner of what is now Turkey. At some point in his family's history, they had acquired Roman citizenship, possibly after military service. But it was in Jerusalem, at the heart of Jewish life and faith, that Saul had received his training in the Jewish law. A Greek, a Roman and a Jew, Paul was something of a cultural hybrid.

Back in Jerusalem after many years in the Gentile world, Paul had been urged by leaders of the Jesus community in Jerusalem to allay suspicions by demonstrating his adherence to Jewish customs (21:17–26). It seems the plan backfired, however, as his presence in the temple provoked a riot (21:27–36). From the Fortress Antonia that towered over the temple, troops poured down to enforce order, and Paul, evidently at the centre of whatever the trouble was, was seized. In the ensuing sequence of events, all three aspects of Paul's identity come into play.

As Paul was being bundled up the steps into the garrison, the senior officer was startled to be addressed by him in very correct Greek: 'May I say something to you?' (21:37). That immediately refuted his assumption that he already knew who he was dealing with. When he allowed Paul to speak to the crowd, there was another surprise. He addressed them in Hebrew: 'Brothers and fathers, listen' (22:1). Whether by 'the Hebrew dialect' Luke means Hebrew or Aramaic is not clear, but it had the effect of hushing the crowd and giving weight to Paul's claim to be indeed one of them, a faithful Jew educated in the scriptures. The third strand emerges later, as the standard interrogation method of flogging a suspect to get at the truth was about to be implemented. Again, Paul asks a polite question: 'Is it legal for you to flog a Roman citizen who is uncondemned?' (22:25). Again, there was consternation and a dramatic change in attitude towards the prisoner.

Greek culture and language; Jewish training and observance; Roman citizenship – all those strands of Paul's hybrid identity and formation were woven into who he became and what he was equipped to do in the service of Christ. And as Paul told his story, it found its coherence and purpose in relation to Jesus' story (22:3–21).

6 The empire and the kingdom

Acts 28:11–31

To some readers, the ending of Acts seems anticlimactic. Why does Luke not complete the story and tell us the outcome of Paul's anticipated trial in Rome? Should there have been a subsequent volume, or at least a chapter 29? This, however, is to miss Luke's point. Compare the beginning and the ending of the Acts narrative. It starts with Jesus, through the Holy Spirit, giving evidence of the reality of his risen life and teaching about the kingdom of God (1:1–3). It concludes with Paul, in alignment with the Holy Spirit's revelation through scripture and with the boldness that is a mark of the Spirit's empowering, testifying to Jesus and teaching about the kingdom of God (vv. 23–31).

This *inclusio* indicates the central focus of the book. It is on the interconnected themes of Jesus, the kingdom and the witness and empowering of the Holy Spirit.

As anticipated in Jesus' promise in 1:8, the witness has been carried out from Jerusalem, at the heart of the faith of Israel, to the world beyond. Now it has reached Rome, at the centre of the empire that dominated the world in which the New Testament events were played out.

There is a breathtaking audacity here. Jesus is declared to be Lord in the very city from which Caesar claimed universal dominion; the kingdom of God is announced not by a conquering general but by a prisoner who to all appearances is subject to the authority of the regime. This, too, is Luke's point. Whether met with approval or opposition, the message about Jesus has proved unstoppable and the kingdom community has continued to grow. This has been affirmed by a series of summary statements (2:47; 6:7; 9:31; 12:24; 19:20). This final summary looks forward: 'This salvation of God has been sent to the Gentiles [or 'nations']; they will listen' (v. 28). This is not the end of the story, but the launching point for a further phase of mission to the nations.

There is a footnote to this stunning image of the message of the kingdom being unleashed at the heart of the empire. It took place in rented accommodation, probably a tenement apartment in Rome's Jewish quarter (vv. 16, 23). Who paid the rent? Then, as now, mission in strategic locations requires not only the bold messenger but also those unknown supporters who provide the means for mission practitioners to live and minister in those contexts.

Guidelines

- Do you agree that, in the absence of some special sign, it can be enough simply to act out of selfless concern for others? If so, what will you do?

- Reflect on your experiences of doors closing. Have any been a 'not yet' or a 'not you'? What does it look like to keep on journeying after such an experience?

- Think of your church and its local witness, discipling and community life. Now think again, but instead of picturing a church building, imagine the households of members of the church community as the loci of worship, learning, sharing and mission. What would be different?

- Go for a walk around your neighbourhood. What do you see, hear and feel? Are there indications of a spiritual quest, or of hopes and beliefs that you can affirm?

- Spend unhurried time in a place where there are people – a square, a shopping centre, a market. Practise attentiveness to people and place, and availability for interaction.

- Pray for Christians who live, serve and witness in daunting urban contexts, that they will be assured that among the anonymous masses God actually has many people.

- Consider the elements that make up your own identity and that have shaped who you are. How might each of those resource your unique participation in the mission of God?

- List any circumstances that seem to obstruct your participation in the mission of God. Reflect on the final scene of the book of Acts, and Paul's testimony that, no matter what his personal circumstances, 'the word of God is not chained' (2 Timothy 2:8–10; compare Philippians 1:12–14).

Reading God's word today

David Dewey

'When I use a word,' Humpty Dumpty said in rather a scornful tone, 'it means just what I choose it to mean – neither more nor less.'

'The question is,' said Alice, 'whether you *can* make words mean so many different things.' (Lewis Carroll, *Through the Looking Glass*, 1872)

Christians across all traditions deeply desire to take God's words seriously. And those words are found in scripture. But we don't have to look far to see how different traditions and approaches can read different meanings into scripture. It's one reason we have so many denominations. We would like to think *we* are the ones reading the Bible in the right way. But at the same time, our brothers and sisters in Christ believe they are doing exactly the same!

Examples abound of differing biblical interpretations over doctrinal, ecclesiastical and pastoral issues. And often they all claim biblical justification. Take, for instance, the variety of doctrine when it comes to human free will, predestination or the end times. What of church governance? Does authority reside in a bishop (as with Roman Catholics and Anglicans), in an eldership (Presbyterians) or with the local congregation (Baptists)? More sensitive still, where do we stand in the ongoing debates over gender roles and human sexuality in church, family and society?

Whether we like it or not, we all read the Bible through one lens or another, which will be coloured by many things: what we have been taught, the church tradition in which we stand, the views of our favourite preachers and writers, our life experiences, our educational backgrounds, our personalities and more.

We will not, in a week, solve the questions that face us as we seek to be faithful in understanding and applying scripture. But we can seek out some principles and become more aware of the personal preferences and prejudices we bring to our Bible reading. Paula Gooder, former Theologian in Residence for Bible Society, suggests that instead of trying to find the one *right* way to read the Bible, we can learn to read it *well*.

Unless otherwise stated, Bible quotations are from the New Revised Standard Version (Anglicised).

1 Finding Christ in all of scripture

Luke 24:13–35

As a young Christian, I used to think that if I could meet Jesus face-to-face I would be so much clearer about what I believed. But two disciples, trudging wearily home to Emmaus carrying with them the despairing thought that Jesus was dead and gone, are surprised to encounter the risen Lord. They go on to discover that even they still very much need the scriptures.

Jesus, as he walks unrecognised beside them, 'interpreted to them the things about himself in all the scriptures' (v. 27). These 'scriptures' are the Christian Old Testament, divided by Jews into three sections: the Law, the Prophets and the Writings (compare 24:44; Psalms form the first and largest book in the Writings).

This passage, near the end of the gospel, creates a bookend with Luke 4:16–21, in which Jesus similarly claims that he is the centrepiece of God's words to humankind and is the one in whom scripture finds its fulfilment.

As Christians we read scripture, first and foremost, to meet the risen, living Christ in the present. He, together with the meaning of his death and resurrection, is revealed in its pages. We note how the Emmaus two report how their hearts burned within them as he opened the scriptures to them (v. 32).

But we also note that Jesus was not recognised by them until he later blessed and broke the bread in their home (vv. 30–31). This phrasing is clearly intended to remind us of the events of the last supper and the church's ongoing eucharistic practice. Word and sacrament always go together. Christ can be found in scripture by any individual, but he is most fully and perfectly revealed as we read and study those scriptures in the company of God's people as we fellowship and worship together.

Realising this is a great leveller. While individual scholars, great teachers and biblical experts all have important contributions to make, scripture and its interpretation belong first to the church. Scripture is best read and applied by humble and faithful followers of Christ, meeting week by week in his name as we offer him the worship of our hearts and lives.

2 Grown in the right soil

We stay with Luke's gospel to consider this most fundamental of all Jesus' parables – the parable of the sower and soils. It is the only parable in Luke to which Jesus appends his own explanation.

Often, this parable is applied to evangelistic contexts as a means of explaining the different responses we can encounter in preaching the gospel to the unchurched or the unbeliever. Doubtless it is applicable in this setting, but over the years I have come to see that it is equally applicable to longstanding churchgoers and Christian believers, myself included. How many challenging sermons have I heard only to realise months later that I have made little or no progress towards meeting my initially good and enthusiastic intentions?

The parable describes the forces pulling every Christian away from a full and obedient response to God's word contained in scripture. These forces can be equated with the believer's three traditional enemies – the world, the flesh and the devil – the enemies against which our baptismal vows remind us we must fight. The devil snatches the word away and makes us deaf to it; the flesh is content with a short-lived, shallow response; and the world, with its alternative attractions of 'cares and riches and pleasures of life' (v. 14), entices us towards a compromised, half-hearted faith.

It is good to be concerned that we are interpreting scripture in the right way. But where does right interpretation get us unless it is accompanied by right application? Better by far to understand a little and apply it well than to understand a lot but to apply it inconsistently or not at all. As Mark Twain put it, 'It ain't the parts of the Bible that I can't understand that bother me, it's the parts that I do understand.'

James (1:22–25) provides us with a stark warning: 'Be doers of the word, and not merely hearers who deceive themselves. For if any are hearers of the word and not doers, they are like those who look at themselves in a mirror; for they look at themselves and, on going away, immediately forget what they were like. But those who look into the perfect law, the law of liberty, and persevere, being not hearers who forget but doers who act – they will be blessed in their doing.'

3 The inspiration of scripture

2 Timothy 3:10—4:5

The apostle Paul's charge to a younger pastor provides us with a passage that is often the first to be cited in any discussion on the authority and inspiration of scripture.

Paul's central concern is that, faced with a combination of outright hostility, society's slide into godless living and the rise of erroneous doctrine in the church (probably Ephesus), Timothy and other believers may find the foundation of their faith being shaken. And Paul's answer is that those who are grounded in the scriptures need not just survive, but also can thrive in their faith.

Building on what we 'unearthed' yesterday from the parable of the soils, we now discover deeper detail about how scripture functions in the life of the Christian disciple. First, scripture is 'able to instruct you' (v. 15; or, in other translations, 'makes us wise') for salvation through faith in Christ Jesus. It is important to read the whole sentence. It is not knowing scripture that saves, but faith in Christ. The biblically illiterate believer has as much claim on heaven as the greatest Bible scholar. But it is the student of scripture that is most likely to grow in faith.

The language of 3:16 is the language of the classroom and thus of discipleship. Scripture promotes both right belief and right behaviour, and does each of these two things through positive and negative approaches. With regards to belief, scripture teaches the truth and refutes error; and with regards to behaviour, scripture trains us in right ways of living while simultaneously challenging our wrong behaviours and habits.

A key principle in reading scripture wisely or well is to read in context. Most Christians in the west will read these verses as applying to them individually. While personal Bible knowledge and Bible reading have an important place (and as a *Guidelines* reader, I assume you agree!), Paul in this letter is encouraging Timothy in the tasks of preaching and pastoral care. Teaching, reproof, correction and training in righteousness are all pastoral functions of scripture to which the church is called. Clergy will have a leading role in this pastoral application of scripture, but the task is far from confined to the clergy: proficiently using scripture to build up one another as disciples of Christ is a key calling of all church members, lay and ordained.

4 The Spirit gives life

2 Corinthians 2:12—3:18

The apostle Paul takes an Old Testament story and gives it a new twist. The story is that of Moses, who received from God the legally binding terms and conditions of the covenant (Exodus 31) and, more specifically, whose face shone whenever he was praying before God (Exodus 34:29–35).

From this starting point, Paul defends his apostleship as a minister of a new, more glorious, life-giving covenant, written not on stone but in the human heart. He insists that while 'the letter kills… the Spirit gives life' (3:6). And 'where the Spirit of the Lord is, there is freedom' (3:17).

If so, how much freedom do we have in reinterpreting and applying scripture in today's changing and challenging world? Is it enough to claim that we are in line with general biblical principles or that we are working with the grain of scripture even when we choose to overturn traditional interpretations of particular passages?

To put it another way: must we take the letter of scripture as unchanging, timeless truth, or can we argue that, because some passages are culturally specific, we are free to reinterpret them for our own contemporary culture and according to how we feel 'led by the Spirit'? A highly sensitive example would be our understanding of human sexuality and the biblical definition of marriage.

There is no simple answer, but looking again at the passage before us, we can see the question of motive is all-important for Paul. Apostle though he is, he insists that as a humble servant of God he is acting in all sincerity; and he knows he is answerable to God for his ministry of God's word (2:16).

Against a situation in which others are peddling God's word for fame or fortune, power or prestige, the passage indicates there are several moral tests that can be applied as to whether we are reading scripture well: is the gospel of grace promoted? Are lives transformed (starting with our own)? Is Christ glorified? Are we advancing ourselves and seeking praise from others, or are we commended by God?

5 'But I say to you...'

Here, we have another example of the reinterpretation of scripture. And this time it is Jesus who is commenting on a list of Old Testament commands. But again, it raises the question of how far we can go in reinterpreting scripture for today. There are important points to note.

First, this is Jesus speaking, and he is inaugurating his new covenant. We are not Jesus, and unlike Jesus, to whom the Bible bears witness, we always sit under scripture, never over it.

Second, we notice that we must distinguish between the scriptures themselves and later interpretations that have added layers of meaning. Part of Jesus' purpose (as, for example, his comments on anger and divorce) is to correct the Pharisees' distortion of the law. We may find great value in the insight of later traditions (Evangelical, Reformed, Catholic, etc.), but sometimes we need to peel away the layers and go back to Bible basics.

Third, notice that Jesus has not come to abolish, but to fulfil the law. He both fulfilled the requirements of the law in his own person – the only person ever to have done so – and is the central figure to whom all scripture points.

Fourth, Jesus both internalises and raises the standards required of us. The bad news is that he sees all our shortcomings. But the good news is that he has given us an example to follow and his indwelling Holy Spirit to make possible what the law, working externally by itself, could never make possible.

And finally, we notice the context (that all-important word again). This passage is set within the sermon on the mount. Is Jesus offering us law or grace? In the Old Testament, blessings followed those who kept the law and curses were pronounced on those who didn't (Deuteronomy 27—28). Jesus' sermon on the mount, however, begins with the pronouncement of blessing on the poor in spirit. With the help of the Spirit, we strive to keep Jesus' commands not in order to acquire God's approval and saving grace, but in gratitude for the fact they are already ours in Christ.

6 Faith, hope and love

1 Corinthians 13

Not only is love the fulfilling of the law (compare Romans 13:10), but learning to live in love towards God and neighbour is also the object and purpose of our Bible study. And this is the paramount test of whether we are reading the Bible well: through our interaction with scripture, alone or with others, are we growing as disciples of Jesus Christ? To read the Bible well is to grow in love.

Early Christians, most notably Origen (c. 184–253), frequently struggled with reading the Old Testament as Christian scripture. In response, they adopted figurative ways of interpreting the Bible. Alongside the face-value meaning of scripture, they saw several layers that they termed the 'spiritual' senses of scripture.

Admittedly, problems arose when these figurative or allegorical meanings became over-inventive and were cut adrift from the plain, historical meaning of the text. Before we can ask what the Holy Spirit is saying to us today from scripture, we must first seek to ascertain what meaning the original author intended the original reader to take from the text.

However, corresponding to these 'spiritual' senses, early devotional writers utilised the three Christian virtues of faith, hope and love as a way of interrogating scripture. Mark Strauss in *How to Read the Bible in Changing Times* (Baker, 2011) develops a series of questions addressed to those who seek to reflect the nature and purpose of God, questions that spring naturally from these three virtues. Here they are:

- Faith: How does this passage inform our understanding of the nature of God and his purpose for the world?
- Hope: What does this passage teach us about who we ought to be in our attitudes and character?
- Love: What does this passage teach us about what we ought to do in our goals and actions?

Using this framework can offer a simple and fruitful approach to personal and collective Bible reading. Why not take some time in quiet, and prayerfully apply Strauss' set of questions to the passage we have read today?

Guidelines

Reading the Bible well and interpreting scripture faithfully is both an art and a science. And it is best done not only as an individual, but first and foremost collectively from within the family of faith as it seeks to offer worship and bear witness to Christ.

As Mark Strauss indicates, there are rules that apply. What are the immediate and wider contexts of the passage before me? And where does it fit in the larger story of scripture? What kind of writing (or genre) is this? And what do I understand to be the original author's purpose in the light of the passage's historical context and literary style?

And we've seen that there are other useful questions we can bring to the text, as well as limits to our freedom in how far we can go in reapplying the timeless truths of scripture to our changing culture.

But as well as discovering these 'rules' and learning to apply appropriate guidelines wisely and consistently, we continually need to look at our hearts. Are we motivated by wanting to be right or by wanting to learn and grow as disciples of Christ? Is God's word bearing fruit in my thinking, my character, my attitudes, my actions?

Let Psalm 1 have the last word: 'Happy are those who delight in the law of the Lord, who meditate on it day and night: they are like trees planted by streams of water, yielding their fruit in season, prospering in all that they do' (paraphrased).

FURTHER READING

Nigel Beynon and Andrew Sach, *Dig Deeper: Tools to unearth the Bible's treasure* (IVP, 2010).

Gordon Fee and Douglas Stuart, *How to Read the Bible Book by Book* (Zondervan, 2002).

Gordon Fee and Douglas Stuart, *How to Read the Bible for All Its Worth* (Zondervan, 2003).

Stanley Gundry and Gary Meadors (eds), *Four Views on Moving beyond the Bible to Theology* (Zondervan, 2009).

Howard I. Marshall, *Beyond the Bible: Moving from scripture to theology* (Baker, 2004).

Mark L. Strauss, *How to Read the Bible in Changing Times* (Baker, 2011).

The role of the Holy Spirit in the communication process

Kate Bruce

I have often pondered the relationship between human skill and divine initiative in communication. Scripture and experience suggest that the Spirit works in the communicator as well as in the receiver. The Spirit is well able to counteract the interference that can hinder communication. Some comfort here for the wobbly preacher!

This week's notes explore the Spirit's role at the heart of all effective communication. God uses human skill but is not limited by it. He takes our flawed efforts and breathes life into them such that they speak powerfully in multivalent ways. One of the most powerful sermons I gave came at the end of a week in which the anticipated preparation time had been wiped out by demands. I found myself in a place I counsel fledgling preachers to flee from: Saturday evening and a blank page. In spite of inadequate preparation, God honoured my attempt under pressure and the result was more powerful than I could have anticipated. This is not an argument for inadequate preparation, just a reminder that the Holy Spirit is the master communicator and he never abandons his apprentices.

This week, we will begin by considering speech as divine gift. We will examine the day of Pentecost, noting that the Spirit enabled communication between languages as well as inspiring Peter to bring scripture alive in his bold and effective sermon. The gift of the divine Spirit in Exodus 31 reminds us that art can speak powerfully in multimedia forms. We can and should expect to hear God speaking across all platforms: from pulpits to portraits; Bible studies to blogs; icons to Instagram. John's gospel shows that the Spirit communicates intimately in advocacy, comfort and teaching, as well as communicating to those who don't believe in him; unbelief is not a barrier to God's communication, worth remembering in mission initiatives. Often, when we run into odd coincidences or strange dreams, the Holy Spirit is at work, as Peter and Cornelius discovered. The Spirit broods over all our communication, equipping those he calls to tell in myriad ways the story of God's deep love for the world. Various other biblical passages are referenced, in brackets, in the notes below for those who wish to explore that particular note in more detail.

Unless otherwise stated, Bible quotations are from the New Revised Standard Version (Anglicised).

1 'Who gives speech to mortals?'

Exodus 4:10–17

Moses is very reluctant to take up God's offer to tell Pharaoh to release his Israelite slaves. He throws up a series of objections, including the argument, loosely translated, 'I'm rubbish with words.' Many a new preacher might identify with this fear. God's response to Moses (v. 11) is profoundly encouraging: 'Who gives speech to mortals?' (Not a bad inscription for the inside of a pulpit.) With this comes the assurance that God will teach Moses what to say, with the powerful statement, 'I will be with your mouth' (v. 12). Moses' response, 'Please send someone else' (v. 13), while honest, is short-sighted. The one who has promised to give him the words to say is he who spoke and it was so (Genesis 1:3), the creative Word who brought all things into being (John 1:1–5) and the one whose word caused a dead man to vacate his own tomb (John 11:43). God's word is powerful. Isaiah used the image of rain and snow watering the earth, causing plants to grow, feeding the people, to communicate the efficacy of the divine word. It always accomplishes God's purpose (Isaiah 55:10–11).

Jesus assured his disciples that in a tight spot, in this case called before religious and political authorities, 'the Holy Spirit will teach you at that very hour what you ought to say' (Luke 12:12). God never changes. He who tuned Moses' tongue, gave words to Jeremiah (Jeremiah 1:6–10) and tutored early disciples in apologetics continues to give speech to all called to speak God's words, in whatever context – school assembly, board room, comedy club, council chamber, pulpit, meal table – wherever. The question 'Who gives speech to mortals?' acts as an anxiety-soother as well as an ego-tamer. Moses describes himself as 'slow of speech and slow of tongue' (v. 10) and yet his daunting mission to make demands of Pharaoh is ultimately successful.

Humanly, this was an impossible gig, but with God nothing is impossible (Luke 1:37). Let's be honest; sometimes after a sermon or speech that soars, we see the human ego preening like a peacock. It's worth remembering, then, that however eloquent the words and however brilliant the performance – the breath comes from God, who gives speech to mortals.

2 The Holy Spirit: infilling and outpouring

Acts 2:1–41

Undoubtedly, the day of Pentecost is strange. Luke describes a hurricane inside the house where the disciples are and tongues of flame resting on each one. Interestingly, Luke doesn't dwell on these phenomena; he focuses attention on the effect of being filled with the Holy Spirit. This spiritual infilling leads to a linguistic outpouring, as God reveals himself afresh. In this outpouring, we see words spoken in one language being heard in another; a man who had once hidden himself communicates a public message with power and punch; and ancient written texts pulse with new life.

In *The Hitchhiker's Guide to the Galaxy*, there is reference to the 'babel fish'. You put this handy creature into your ear and instantly you understand any language. In the Acts reading, it is as though everyone has their own babel fish! The message concerning 'God's deeds of power', spoken in Aramaic with a Galilean accent, is heard by a range of language speakers in their mother tongues. This event happened during the Festival of Weeks, a Jewish festival of covenant renewal. Through the spiritual infilling of the disciples comes a linguistic outpouring concerning the nature of the God of the covenant. For some, the Spirit's words stir up deep desire for God; amazed and perplexed, they ask questions. Inevitably, some sneer and turn away. It's always the way. We are free to move towards or away from God, to listen to our deepest desire or to mute it.

The effects of the infilling of the Holy Spirit are clear as Peter stands up to speak to the crowds. The last time we saw Peter in Luke's narrative, he was giving a speech to 120 believers (Acts 1:15–17); prior to that, we saw him at the empty tomb (Luke 24:12); and just before that, we saw that 'he went out and wept bitterly' as the accusing cockerel crowed (Luke 22:62). Peter has come a long way. Our impetuous friend is now boldly proclaiming the gospel to an audience of thousands. He weaves in references to Hebrew scripture, ancient written texts inspired by the Spirit now amplifying this new message.

Communication is a spiritual activity. Creative outpouring, in whatever medium, requires spiritual infilling: 'Come, Holy Ghost, our souls inspire.'

3 The Holy Spirit: multimedia communicator

Exodus 31:1–11; 35:30–35

The Holy Spirit is the source of Bezalel's and Oholiab's creative skill, expressed in multimedia communication. They exercise their divine gifts in designing and building, hammering precious metal, embroidering a design or weaving the curtain cloth. The divine gift is expressed when they teach others these skills. Full of God's creative Spirit, they help others to make a place of multimedia encounter with God.

The Holy Spirit works in multimedia. See God with a paintbrush, dotting spots on the ladybird's back. Listen, God is playing tenor sax, singing creation in chords. Smell the loamy richness of newborn earth. Taste the homely flavour of bread, baked and broken. Touch the soft hair of the baby's head: God's glory in skin, the creative risk of God.

In God's image, we are called to orientate all our creativity on communicating God to the world. When we do this, the encounter-place is born. Such artistry is multimedia: from stained-glass work to blues singing; from exquisite embroidery to the thought-provoking blog.

In the power of the Holy Spirit, *artistic or not*, we are all weavers, welders, writers, singers and painters. He weaves his prayers around a troubled situation and holds the cloth before God. She expresses her objections to unjust government policy in a letter to her MP. He shapes a sermon designed to 'sustain the weary with a word' (Isaiah 50:4). She sings an aria of practical care in visiting the sad and sick. They paint a scene of love around their kitchen table. The tabernacle is created; the place of encounter made.

I imagine the Spirit speaking: 'Oh my people! Do you really think I want a two-dimensional religion of forelock-tugging automatons, dull and dutiful? I call you to a life of jazz riffs and blues chords, a life of beautiful equations of heart-soaring complexity and touching simplicity. I call you to dance, to quilt, to cook, to paint, to write, to build, to film, to play, to caress the ball into the back of the net… and to do it all for me. My apprentices… come to me, your master craftsman – let's make the place of multimedia encounter.'

4 The Holy Spirit: advocate, comforter and teacher

John 14:15-17, 25-26; 16:7-14

We see deep communication within the Trinity. The Son asks the Father on behalf of the disciples for the Spirit to come. The Father sends the Spirit, who dwells deeply in the disciples, reminding them of all that Jesus has said. The Holy Spirit draws the disciples deeper into the things of God.

Central to the communicative act is an exchange between at least two participants. Where there is only one, there can be no true communication, as there is no one to hear. This is the place of existential loneliness: humanity separated from God. Augustine said, 'Our hearts are restless till they find their rest in you.' The restless heart is lonely and longing, missing deep relationship with God and the fulfilment this brings, and often trying to satisfy the need for such intimacy through other means.

The image of the Spirit of truth, living in the disciple, is one of accessibility, reliability, trust and companionship. John uses the term 'advocate' for the Holy Spirit. An advocate is a backer, a champion, an ally, a comrade, a sponsor and a keen supporter. An advocate offers comfort, warmth and understanding, a cradling place for the restless heart. The Holy Spirit expresses advocacy and comfort in the form of teaching, guiding and reminding, keeping the beloved on the right path. We experience the work of the Spirit in the inner nudge, the prompt to pray, the creative impulse, the scriptural earworm that keeps coming to the forefront of the mind and the sense of deep peace and connectedness: all the hallmarks of spiritual consolation.

The Spirit also seeks out the faithless through conviction of the truth of the gospel. In a materialistic world of whiter washing powder, fast food and shrink-fit jeans concepts of sin, righteousness and judgement can seem alien and otherworldly. Gaining a new vision about life in the light of God can only come through the communicating conviction of the Spirit, who gives eyes to see and leads the restless heart home – through advocacy, comfort and teaching. The mission of the church is not simply a matter of human effort; it is a work of the Spirit through the attempts of the church. The invocation of God's Spirit is essential to the work of mission.

5 The Holy Spirit: communicating the extraordinary in the ordinary

Acts 10:1–38, 44–48

This passage demonstrates how the communicative agency of the Spirit intersects with the everyday; the extraordinary is earthed in the ordinary and communicated in both image and word. Ordinary people matter in God's plans; Jew and Gentile are agents in God's mission.

We see this when Cornelius, a Gentile with a desire for God, has a clear vision at three o'clock in the afternoon. Specifics matter in this passage. Notice how the angelic message in Acts includes Simon Peter's name, mention of Simon the tanner and the little detail of his house being by the sea. We are told that, at about noon the next day, Peter has his vision of the sheet full of birds, reptiles and other unclean animals, with the command to kill and eat happening three times, the repetition overriding his objections. The timing is perfect: as Peter ponders, Cornelius' men arrive looking for a stranger they only know by name, and the Spirit instructs Peter to go and meet them. From their perspective, Peter comes out of the house coincidentally at the right moment and then announces, rather oddly, 'I am the one you are looking for.' Behind this human meeting, we see the Spirit brooding, engineering the encounter.

Through the local and specific, God's Spirit inaugurates something with universal import. The mission to the Gentiles is launched through ordinary people who are open to extraordinary visions and obedient to the instruction within the visions. Had Peter or Cornelius been mere materialists, they might have dismissed the vision, put it down to lack of sleep and ignored it. However, they are open to God's cutting into their ordinary world, and obedient to the divine command.

How often is the divine voice unheeded because we dismiss it? Think of the times you have acted on an inner prompt to text or pick up the phone and found the timing to have been perfect for the other person, or the occasions when a dream seems particularly prescient. God's communicative Spirit is active and alive in the ordinary. Are we open to this?

6 The Holy Spirit: source of words in a tight spot

Luke 12:11–12; Acts 5:31–40

Luke paints a picture of the Holy Spirit being utterly faithful to his people and giving them the words needed in a tight spot. The image is of the Spirit being right next to the one called to speak up in difficult circumstances.

We see this again and again in scripture, for example with Shiphrah and Puah, the quick-thinking Hebrew midwives (Exodus 1:19), with Moses (Exodus 4:12, 15) and with Jeremiah (Jeremiah 1:6–10). The promise given to Jeremiah that God will give him the words to speak is borne out through the rest of the book that bears his name; his prophecies are powerful words spoken to dangerous people, giving voice to the divine longing for the people to repent and articulating God's anger at their stubbornness.

The same theme pulses through the New Testament; ordinary people are enabled to communicate with power in challenging circumstances. Peter's Pentecost sermon is an example of this. We also see it in Acts 5 when Peter and the apostles stand before the council and are questioned by the high priest concerning their teaching about Jesus. In the face of this hostile crowd, Peter's words are faithful and clear, pointing to their call to obedience to God rather than human authority. It is no coincidence that Gamaliel speaks up with calming wisdom that turns away the violence of the baying crowd. He speaks for God and points the crowd to God, saying, 'If it is of God, you will not be able to overthrow them – in that case you may even be found fighting against God!' (5:39).

God is present where truth is spoken to power, in the word that turns away ferocity and in the message that endures violence for the sake of truth. We see this in Stephen's speech to the high priest and his followers. This is a bold recitation of God's dealings with his people and their responses. The presence of the Holy Spirit frames the sermon, seen in the expression on Stephen's face (Acts 6:15) and the vision that enables him to see beyond their murderous violence, forgiving them at the moment of his martyrdom (Acts 7:55–60). God communicates through his people and the Spirit equips those he calls.

Guidelines

- Moses argues, 'I'm rubbish with words.' What stories do you tell yourself that close down your cooperation with God's Spirit and limit your communicative skill?

- 'Who gives speech to mortals?' is not a bad inscription for the inside of a pulpit. Come up with your own pulpit inscription that would encourage you, or someone you know, in the preaching task.

- We see on the day of Pentecost that an infilling of the Spirit leads to an outpouring of creative power. Pray for a renewed experience of the Spirit in the church and in your own life.

- Bezalel and Oholiab express their communicative skill across many media. Make a list of people you know who communicate God's love and artistry in multimedia forms. How can you encourage them? Does your local church have groups where such creative people can gather and express their gifts together? Is this something you could develop?

- 'An advocate offers comfort, warmth and understanding, a cradling place for the restless heart.' How does your church express the Spirit's comfort and advocacy? How might this be developed?

- Mission involves a series of communicative acts in which human effort serves divine initiative. The invocation of God's Spirit is essential to the work of mission. What mission initiatives are happening through your church and how is prayer underpinning these activities?

- Peter and Cornelius discover God's extraordinary communication in the ordinary everyday. Are you open to experiencing God's word through visions, dreams and odd 'coincidences' or has materialism closed down expectancy?

- Often, what we say about God can be at odds with what our behaviour suggests about our belief. I might believe in theory that God equips those he calls, while experiencing fear and mistrust. Take time to talk with God about your uncertainties and anxieties in communication, and listen to God's response.

Hosea

C.L. Crouch

Apart from the mention of his father's name in this book's heading (1:1), which distinguishes Hosea son of Beeri from the several other Hoseas who appear in the biblical texts, we know next to nothing about the origins or personal circumstances of this prophet. The book's interest in the northern kingdom and the people of Israel leads us to assume that Hosea was himself from the northern kingdom, although the ultimate reception and preservation of the book among the religious writings of the southern kingdom is reflected in the intermittent appearances of Judah in a few places.

The book's heading names four kings of Judah and one of Israel, placing Hosea's message in relation to events of the eighth century BC. A more precise date is difficult to pin down, but a concentration of Hosea's activity in the third quarter of the eighth century is most likely; this would make sense of the book's attention to the implications of rising Neo-Assyrian power in the region.

Unlike with Isaiah and Ezekiel, there is no report of Hosea's call to prophetic ministry; the rarity with which the book employs typical oracular formulae such as 'Thus says the Lord' is also unusual. The meaning of the Hebrew text is frequently opaque, sometimes even indecipherable; a comparison of different translations will show the wide variety of ways in which translators have attempted to make sense of the preserved text. Some of these peculiarities may relate to the book's antiquity; Hosea is generally considered the earliest of the prophets whose oracular utterances were collected into written form. The book is undoubtedly most famous for using marriage as a metaphor for the relationship between God and his people, in a complex and multifaceted exploration of the religious and political implications of the deity's insistence on the people's fidelity to the Lord alone. In both theology and language, Hosea has special resonances with the book of Deuteronomy, including a similar emphasis on the exclusivity of Israel's relationship with Yahweh.

Unless otherwise stated, Bible quotations and headings are from the New Revised Standard Version (Anglicised).

1 The family of Hosea and the restoration of Israel

Hosea 1:2—2:1

The details of Hosea's personal life and its significance as a representation of the relationship between God and Israel have been the subject of endless scrutiny. Other prophets undertake actions with symbolic significance, sometimes even including members of their family – Isaiah gives children symbolic names; Ezekiel is forbidden to mourn his wife; Jeremiah is forbidden even to have one – but few sign-acts demand so much of the prophet as God's command that Hosea 'take for yourself a wife of whoredom and have children of whoredom' (1:2) as symbols of Israel's infidelity to the Lord. Whether Gomer's description as 'a wife of whoredom' means that she was already engaged in promiscuous behaviour, or anticipates her future infidelity, is not clear. Similarly, the children are 'children of whoredom', but at least the first is also said to be born to Hosea (1:3).

Their names signify aspects of God's relationship to Israel. The first, Jezreel ('God sows'), declares that the violence and bloodshed that brought the ruling royal house to the throne (2 Kings 9—10) will soon be repaid upon it. It anticipates condemnation of Israel's political elites, highlighting more strongly than we might expect the importance of Israel's *social* behaviour as a reflection of its faith in the Lord. The second child, a daughter called Lo-ruhamah ('not pitied'), symbolises the exhaustion of the Lord's parental patience with Israel; the Lord has tolerated Israel's bad behaviour long enough. The breakdown of the relationship reaches its climax with the third child, Lo-ammi ('not my people'), whose birth signals the undoing of the covenant relationship between the Lord and Israel (see Exodus 6:7; Leviticus 26:12).

Verse 7 interjects to say that the Lord's abandonment of Israel does not extend to Judah, in the first of several passages that seek to relate Hosea's words to later readers in the southern kingdom. Echoing the condemnation of Israel's violent past, symbolised by the child Jezreel, this promise is grounded in Judah's faith in God, not its military strength.

The negativity heaped upon Israel via Gomer and her children is rescinded at the last moment: the relationship breakdown symbolised by Lo-ammi will be overcome by the Lord's claiming of the people as his children (1:10). The promise that the people of Israel and the people of Judah will be reunited anticipates the punishment of each by deportation and dispersion. The declaration concerning the greatness of Jezreel plays now on its positive aspect: 'God sows' proclaims the source of Israel and Judah's blessings (1:11). God's ultimate mercy is promised: the unpitied will be pitied and those who were not the Lord's people will be 'Ammi' – 'my people' (2:1).

2 Israel's infidelity and punishment

Hosea 2:2–13

Hosea 2 unpacks the metaphor of God's marriage to Israel. Just as Gomer was described in chapter 1 as a whore and her children as the children of whoredom, so chapter 2 now describes Israel (vv. 2, 4–5). This poetry speaks of the time after God and Israel's 'divorce' – after their marital vows have been countermanded by the Lord's declaration that 'she is not my wife, and I am not her husband' (v. 2; echoing the declaration in 1:9 that 'you are not my people and I am not your God'). The vitriol and violence of God's words is shocking: he will humiliate and then kill her (v. 3).

Both the power and the danger of metaphor are apparent here. The passage evokes the deep-rending pain of a betrayed spouse to articulate the grief and the fury of God betrayed by Israel, but in its description of Israel's fate it goes beyond any known ancient punishment for adultery. The rhetorical extremes to which the text goes to describe God's anger are hazardous if taken as licence for such behaviour on the part of human spouses. The violence of God's treatment of Israel derives from the fact that Israel's abandonment of God provokes his reciprocal abandonment of Israel. The description of Israel's punishment for 'adultery' therefore blurs into a more general depiction of the consequences of God's withdrawal of divine protection: the Israelites will be humiliated by their enemies and the natural world will no longer provide for them (v. 3).

It is only with verse 8 that the identity of the one with whom Israel has been unfaithful is revealed. The god Baal was one of the indigenous gods of Canaan, associated especially with weather and therefore with fertility: without the rains, the crops fail and the people die. The people have confused the fecundity given them by the Lord with fecundity given by Baal, therefore (mis)directing their worship towards Baal rather than towards the

Lord (v. 8). The Lord seeks to drive Israel back to himself, withdrawing the blessings he has showered upon Israel (vv. 9, 12) and thereby cutting off the avenues of her pursuit of Baal (vv. 6–7).

3 Israel's redemption

Hosea 2:14–23

The second half of the chapter presents the Lord trying a different tactic: enticing Israel into the wilderness and soliciting her affections through promises of the fruitful land. This proposed sojourn in the wilderness is an allusion to the earliest part of God and Israel's relationship, after God had brought Israel out of slavery in Egypt. With the notable exception of Ezekiel 20, which presents the relationship as a disaster from day one, the wilderness between Egypt and the promised land is prophetically perceived as God and Israel's honeymoon period, in which the young and innocent Israel was newly wed and faithful to the Lord (compare Jeremiah 2–3). The image suggests an attempt to bring the troubled relationship back to its starting place – to begin anew.

As anyone who has been married or in a serious relationship will know, of course, it is impossible ever to erase completely the sins of a relationship's past. Nevertheless, God offers here just such an impossibility: the promise that, with this new beginning, the troubles of God and Israel's past will be forgotten. Even more remarkably, they will not be repeated. The name of Israel's adulterous lover – Baal, 'Lord' – will never more cross her lips; the troublesome ambiguity by which Israel had confused this other deity with her one true Lord and husband will be eradicated.

The Lord's responsibility for Israel's welfare is once more expressed in terms of Israel's relationship with the natural world; this new covenant contrasts with their earlier antagonism (2:3). The threat of humiliation by Israel's enemies will also be abolished. God summons Israel to a new and indestructible relationship, committing himself to righteousness, justice, love, mercy and faithfulness. That the only mention of faithfulness in this idyllic future concerns the Lord's own underscores the forgiveness and forgottenness of the past (v. 20). The passage climaxes with an explicit inversion of the children's rejections from chapter 1: God will sow (Jezreel), will have pity (Lo-ruhamah) and will declare once more that Israel is God's people (Lo-ammi).

4 Further assurances of God's redeeming love

Hosea 3

Unlike chapter 1, in which we heard about Hosea's marriage from the perspective of an anonymous narrator, chapter 3 relates a first-person account of what the Lord asked Hosea to do. There is some uncertainty over whether the unnamed woman of chapter 3 is the same woman named as Gomer in chapter 1. Gomer was called a 'wife of whoredom', suggesting a previous career in sex work, and was explicitly said to have three children, including one born to Hosea. The woman of chapter 3 is described as an adulteress with a lover, implying that she was previously married but not faithful to her spouse, and is instructed by Hosea not to have sex at all, not even with him.

Part of the confusion undoubtedly arises from the ready slippage in these chapters and in other biblical texts between adultery and sex work, especially in passages describing God and Israel's relationship as one involving Israel's infidelity. Whereas we would distinguish sex work and extramarital sex as two quite different activities, with very different motivations, the biblical texts view both as forms of female defiance of male authority, useful and largely interchangeable ways of speaking about Israel's defiance of the Lord's authority.

The symbolic significance of Hosea's female partner is clearer here than it was in chapter 1: Hosea is instructed to love this woman despite her affairs with men who are not her husband, just as the Lord loves Israel despite its affairs with gods who are not its God. The 'many days' without intimacy between Hosea and the woman foreshadow a future in which the Israelites will spend many days without the means by which they are accustomed to communicating with their God: no king, no priest, no prophet.

5 God accuses Israel

Summoning the people to hear the word, chapter 4 marks the beginning of several chapters of poetic oracles. These comprise the majority of the book's message, though they are often overshadowed by chapters 1—3. Like the first three chapters, they contain mostly condemnation and judgement, interspersed with hints of hope and promise, especially in chapters 11 and 14.

There is no clear order or structure to these oracles; they seem rather to be a roughly organised collection associated with the prophet and his ministry, which unpack Israel's faithlessness in more specific and practical terms. The opening indictment of chapter 4 thus echoes the earlier condemnations of Israel's disloyalty and unfaithfulness, which it traces to Israel's ignorance of God. This ignorance manifests itself in various forms of social breakdown, echoing the concerns of the ten commandments: the land is filled with swearing, lying, murder, stealing and adultery (v. 2). The first three reflect the power of the spoken word in the ancient world: in the absence of forensic evidence, to swear an oath falsely could condemn a person to death. Theft and adultery are crimes of covetousness. These religious and social offences are linked directly to the state of nature: because the people do not do as they ought, the land and everything in it suffers. Faithlessness is manifested in failures of fellowship, and in damage to God's creation.

While observing the guilt of the whole community, Hosea identifies Israel's leadership as especially culpable for this grim state of affairs (v. 4). Those responsible for the education of the people and the cultivation of their knowledge of God have failed in their task, with the whole community led astray by the ignorance that results. Rather than recognise and repent of their wrongdoing, however, the leadership intensify it. They take the advantages that accrue to them and make the most of them, abusing their positions of power to pervert the people's behaviour beyond recognition. Hosea's condemnation employs sexualised language for these leaders' misdeeds in a way that is familiar from contemporary English: they prostituted themselves to power for personal gain. Their punishment will be just deserts: though they pervert the purposes of their positions, these attempts will fail.

6 The idolatry of Israel

Hosea 4:11–19

The second half of Hosea 4 addresses more straightforwardly religious offences. Cultic practices in many times and places have involved the use of mind-altering substances; here, Hosea condemns the use of alcohol as a means of opening the mind to God on the grounds that what results is not then understood (compare 1 Corinthians 14:6–19). The dissipation and licentiousness that accompanies drunkenness seems also in view at the end of the passage (v. 18). Severely compounding the offence is that the oracles are not sought from God but from mere idols. The people are misdirecting their devotions, mistaking the pleasantness of shady hilltops as a sign for the power of the gods they worship there.

The prophet employs sexualised language to describe these infidelities, using images of proliferating and perverse sexual practices to articulate the wantonness with which the Israelites are experimenting with other gods. Although many modern translations refer to 'temple prostitutes' (v. 14), a number of recent studies have concluded that there is no evidence for temple prostitutes as a real part of any ancient Israelite or other ancient Near Eastern worship practice. The word *qedeshim* is simply a word for sanctified temple personnel. The image of Israelite men paying for religious sacrifices and sex workers simultaneously, while the Israelite women cavort with abandon, is a rhetorically shocking way of grabbing hearers' attention, by casting their dalliances with other deities in the starkest of terms. It is not a description of actual cultic sex.

Perhaps in an attempt to clarify the remit of the marriage metaphor that dominates these chapters, Hosea emphasises that it is both the Israelite men and the Israelite women who are engaged in these infidelities. Indeed, verse 14 makes the startling declaration that the women will not be punished, for the men's behaviour is just as bad, if not worse. This withholding of judgement presupposes that the ultimate fault for the women's waywardness lies at the feet of their fathers, who ought to have held them in better control, but nevertheless strikes against a double standard in the consequences for male and female immorality.

Gilgal and Bethel (v. 15) were two major cultic centres of the northern kingdom; Hosea's objection to the latter is underscored by its invocation as Beth-aven, 'house of sin', here and in 5:8 and 10:5. In 1 Kings 12, Jeroboam's creation of two golden calves for use in Israelite worship at Bethel and at Dan is described; given Baal's iconographic association with the bull and Hosea's recurring concerns about the Israelites' confusion of the Lord and Baal, illicit Baal worship may be in view again here.

Guidelines

Metaphors provoke the imagination by using one thing to describe something else: the similarities and differences between the two things make us think differently about each. Hosea is the first in a long line of Israelite prophets to use marriage as a metaphor for the relationship between God and Israel. Because of the imperfect match between the two parts of a metaphor, one of the challenges in interpreting them is knowing how far to press the comparison. The relationship between God and Israel is *like* a human marriage, but it is not *really* a human marriage, and we will err if we neglect the differences between them. Pressing every last detail into strict analogical service risks making an inherently fluid and flexible way of speaking about God wooden and awkward.

What *is* clear in these chapters is that illustrating God and Israel's relationship through Hosea's marriage brings into focus the severity of Israel's infidelity to the Lord: if infidelity to one's spouse is morally repugnant, how much more so must be infidelity to God? It is a visceral image of betrayal, and a powerful one. But it is not an unproblematic image. Hosea's use of this metaphor is grounded in a deeply patriarchal construction of marriage; it assumes an inequality between the man and the woman that mirrors the inequality between God and Israel. When marriage is conceived as an equal partnership, the way that the metaphor provokes the imagination changes.

There is also an important distinction between using a historically specific form of human marriage to speak about God's relationship with humanity, and the use of God's relationship with humanity to legitimate a historically specific form of human marriage. Hosea's purpose is to provoke the Israelites into recognising the severity of their betrayal of God, not to comment on appropriate forms of human marriage.

Finally, we must recognise that the blurring of God's punitive action against Israel as wife into God's punitive action against Israel as land and nation has created a depiction of God's relationship with his wife that is troublingly violent. This must not be taken as licence for domestic violence. The limits of the metaphor must be respected; although Hosea may be enjoined to love his wife unconditionally, in imitation of the way that God loves Israel, there is no mistaking Hosea for God. As the promises of chapter 2 make clear, God offers something to Israel that cannot be replicated in a human relationship: the possibility of a completely new beginning. Though powerful, the metaphor of God's relationship with Israel can only go so far.

1 Impending judgement on Israel and Judah

Hosea 5

Much of this chapter constitutes variations on previous themes. Again, the elites of the country are singled out: priests and king, as well as the 'house of Israel' (v. 1).

Mizpah was a borderlands site in the region of Benjamin, between Samaria and Jerusalem. It is associated with the prophet Samuel's summons to battle (1 Samuel 7; 10) and would later become the provincial capital of the Babylonians after their conquest of Judah in 586 BC (Jeremiah 40—41; 2 Kings 25). The word means 'watchtower'. Mount Tabor, at the eastern end of the Jezreel Valley, is associated with Deborah's defeat of Sisera (Judges 4). Its location and these two sites' associations with battles suggests a poetic variation on the condemnation of Israel for political violence in 1:4–5.

The heights implied by the 'watchtower' and Mount Tabor are joined by a reference to the depths of Israel's offences in verse 2, emphasising the pervasive nature of Israel's sin – it may be found everywhere, from the peaks to the valleys.

Ephraim was one of the sons of Joseph and the eponymous ancestor of the tribe of Ephraim. The tribe's dominance among the Israelites meant that it could be used as an alternative name for Israel as a whole, as in verse 3. Pride is the stumbling block that keeps Ephraim/Israel from returning to the Lord: as long as they refuse to admit they have a problem, the problem cannot be fixed (vv. 5–6).

Verses 3–4 contrast God's knowledge of Israel with Israel's ignorance of God. Verses 8–15 describe the consequences of Israel's refusal to reform. The final form of the text moves easily between the fate of the northern kingdom, which is most immediately in view for Hosea, and the fate that would later befall the southern kingdom; biblical writers came to understand the latter as a consequence of Judah's failure to heed the lessons of the Lord's dealings with the north (compare 2 Kings 17). The passage also explains that God's judgement on Israel will take the form of national political disaster: the raucous alarms of verse 8 warn of an invading army. Mistaking this looming catastrophe for mere human intrigue, Ephraim races to the Assyrian king for protection.

2 A call to repentance

Hosea 6:1–3

God's insurmountable power is at work; no human king – not even the mighty king of Assyria – can free the Israelites from God's judgement. Only Israel's return to the Lord can bring about restoration, for it is the Lord who has brought about their present distress. The declaration in verse 1 is a statement of God's absolute power: in the Lord's hands are both blessing and curse. Though the Lord is the author of devastating anguish and suffering, the Lord will return to salve the wounds.

This breadth and depth in God's involvement in human affairs, encompassing joyful blessings but also the most painful grief, can be difficult to swallow for Christians raised on a placidly benevolent image of the deity, taught that God wants us to be happy always and only. The prophets remind us of God's complexity as well as the complexity of our relationship with God. Our vision is short-sighted, hindered by human foibles and limitations. Like a parent's perspective to that of a child, God's sight goes far beyond ours.

In the wider frame of Hosea's marriage metaphor, the danger is that this depiction of God can be transmuted into the language of an abuser, cajoling a broken spouse (or child) back into a destructive relationship with promises of better behaviour in future. Again, we must be mindful of the limitations of metaphor. Although we frequently anthropomorphise God – describing God in human terms as we try to understand that which is beyond human experience – and Genesis 1 describes us as made in the image of God, we are not God. As an ethical model, *imitatio Dei* – the imitation of God – is thus not a carte blanche for us to act like miniature deities. God may do things that we may not.

The progressive parallelism of verse 2 ('after two days... on the third day') is a common Hebrew rhetorical device, put to use also by the prophet Amos (Amos 1:3—2:8) and in Proverbs (Proverbs 30:15–31). For the Christian reader, these verses call to mind the reconciling work of Christ achieved in the days between Maundy Thursday and Easter Sunday.

3 Impenitence of Israel and Judah

Hosea 6:4—7:7

God's despair at the people is the lamentation of a parent at a loss with a recalcitrant child. The people are inconstant in their affections, turning hither and thither from one deity to the next. The Lord has sent warning through the prophets, but the people have not heeded it. Their refusal to listen condemns them; they cannot claim ignorance of their offence, for the prophets have told them of it, time and time again. What more can God do to instruct them? We think of the prophetic voices in our own lives, calling out again and again to bring us to God and to obedience to God's will. What prophets do we ignore?

Adam (6:7) is not the man in Eden but an allusion to the people's entry into the promised land. Joshua 3 describes how the people crossed over the Jordan River near a place called Adam; Hosea contends that the people had turned against God already by that early stage in the relationship.

Gilead and Shechem (6:8–9) signify Israelite territory on either side of the Jordan: Gilead on the east, Shechem on the west. The offences on the road to Shechem are especially grievous because they take advantage of the people's faith: the priests murder pilgrims on their way to the sacred site. The trust placed by the people in their religious leaders has been betrayed. We may compare the outcry upon discovery that a priest or pastor has taken advantage of a parishioner in some way.

But the problem here is not only with the leadership; God seeks to restore the people but finds their superficial piety merely a thin veneer over their rotten interiors (6:11—7:1). Like Amos, Hosea protests against rituals undertaken mindlessly, without rightness of heart (6:6; compare Amos 5:21–25). The people expect the motions of worship to absolve them of their crimes, but God knows their public deeds and their private thoughts; the Lord is not deceived.

The second half of this section turns its attention to the people's political offences. The litany begins with native politics: though Samaria's sycophants may please the human king with their lies and treachery, their perfidy proves the foundation for nothing short of treason (7:2–7; compare 2 Kings 15).

4 Futile reliance on the nations

Hosea 7:8–16

It is no wonder that Israel, suffering from such internal upheaval and chaos, is taken advantage of by others. Verse 11 describes the willy-nilly vacillations of the Israelite kings between the major powers to the east and south. The kings place their trust everywhere save where they ought. They trust in their own strength and in the strength of the kings of Egypt and Assyria, but not in the Lord.

Israel's political blunders take place in the shadow of the Assyrian empire whose king, Tiglath-Pileser III, sought to expand the empire's reach far beyond its Mesopotamian heartland. Although Israel spent much of the second half of the eighth century BC attempting to evade Assyrian domination, the cause would prove futile. Hosea mocks the frantic pleas of Israel's ambassadors to Egypt, babbling incoherently in their desperation for protection from Assyria (v. 16). None of Israel's machinations acknowledge the divine power to which all these human activities are subject. The Israelites believe their problem to be Assyrian power, but the real power driving Assyria's expansion is the Lord's, who is using these foreign powers to illuminate for his people the consequences of their disobedience.

Once more, the offence for which the people are to be punished is theological: verse 14 describes foreign religious practices aimed at extracting promises of fertility from other gods. Hosea assumes an interweaving of the religious and the political, based especially on a belief in the power of God over all spheres of human existence. The Lord is the ultimate authority over Israel; Israel's self-subjection to miscellaneous foreign authorities is thus a contravention of its rightful submission to the Lord alone. Although modern pluralist democracies treat the connection between religion and state much more loosely, Hosea's insight remains potent. Our political behaviours are not walled off in some separate sphere, apart from and of no interest to God. We are accountable for our behaviour in this sphere as in all parts of our existence. Treachery and lies are abhorrent wherever they occur.

5 Israel's apostasy

The condemnations of this chapter concern the manifold forms of Israel's overweening pride. Rather than submit themselves to the Lord's sovereign power, the Israelites have arrogated the power of kingship to themselves, choosing leaders of their own making rather than those appointed with the appropriate gifts. They have similarly appropriated the power to make gods – but, being made of mere metals, these cannot save but rather doom.

The worship of inanimate objects rather than the living God harks back to the sin of the wilderness generation, who lost faith and implored Aaron to make for them a golden calf (Exodus 32). Here, the calf of Samaria represents the storm and fertility god Baal, who once more poses a temptation to Israel. Baal's inability to live up to expectations is unpacked in verse 7; the Israelites have placed their faith in vanity and nothingness, which will accordingly produce nothing but disorder and chaos.

Again, we see the intimate connection between bad faith and bad politics, as Hosea pans out from the domestic agricultural consequences of the Israelites' religious failures to bring into view the international political consequences: having placed its trust in false gods, Israel is defenceless against the machinations of foreign power (vv. 8–10). Promises of loyalty and service to foreign kings cannot replace the security of loyalty and service to the Lord.

The final section returns once more to Israel's cultic waywardness, beginning with its facile understanding of sacrifice (v. 11). Merely going through the motions does not achieve the desired results; Israel's priorities are all wrong. Amos made a similar complaint about Israel's religious practices (Amos 4—5): mindless performance of prescribed rituals is not what the Lord desires. Verse 12 hints, intriguingly, at an early written form of ritual instructions for the right worship of the Lord. Such references to the law are rare in the prophetic texts.

The ultimate consequence of Israel's turning from the Lord to other gods is that the Lord will take Israel back where he found them, namely, to Egypt. Whether Hosea initially envisioned an actual return of the Israelites to Egypt or was speaking rhetorically of their looming dispersal and dissolution at the hands of the Assyrians is unknown.

6 Punishment for Israel's sin

Hosea 9

Hosea 9 resumes the adultery/prostitution imagery but otherwise continues with similar themes. The favours Israel pays out will gain nothing but suffering.

The threat of exile is expanded more broadly here than in the previous chapter: the symbolic return to Egypt, undoing Israel's genesis as a people, appears alongside the more pragmatic threat of deportation by Assyria (v. 3) and dispersal among the nations (v. 17). In the course of its expansion outward from Mesopotamia, the Neo-Assyrian empire made extensive use of deportation as a policy of imperial control. Those who refused to submit to the empire's authority were carted off to some distant part of the empire, where their seditious efforts lacked an audience. In the process, the Assyrians effected the movement of vast numbers of people across the ancient Near East. Hosea's awareness of these policies locates his prophetic oracles firmly in the second half of the eighth century BC, after the accession of Tiglath-Pileser III, who was the first Neo-Assyrian king to attempt to annex the western territories. Hosea interprets the rise of this great earthly power as a reflection of the Lord's ultimate authority, seeing in the Assyrian threat the means by which God has resolved to punish Israel for its betrayal.

The prophets come in for particular scrutiny in the middle part of the chapter (vv. 7–9). The role of the prophet is to speak the divine word to the people, watching over them like a protective sentinel to warn them when they are in danger of going astray. Israel's prophets have not merely failed at their task but worked actively to subvert it, setting traps for the people in lieu of warnings to avoid them. The reference to Gibeah in verse 9 is probably an allusion to the horrors recounted by a later author in Judges 19—21. Then, too, the offences were so great as to warrant near-total destruction.

The second half of the chapter (vv. 10–17) quashes the hope promised by the prospect of a new generation; the children already born will die and there will be no more to come. Though the Israelites have turned to Baal for fertility, it is the Lord who holds sway over both life and death.

Guidelines

The prophets see faith and politics as intimately intertwined. Faced with the destruction of the southern kingdom of Judah in the sixth century BC, the prophet Ezekiel would speak vividly of the king of Babylon as the mercenary arm of the Lord's wrath, working out in the violent devastation and depredation of warfare the consequences for the Israelites' failure to be loyal to their one true God. Though less systematically expressed, Hosea anticipates similar consequences for Israel's disloyalty.

The logic of this militarised form of punishment is rooted in the overlapping conceptual spheres of human and divine royal authority. Human kings frequently used treaties and loyalty oaths to bind their subordinates to them, seeking to assure that they would not turn to another king for support by threatening an imaginative variety of nasty consequences – typically these included plague and famine for the land, deportation for the people and death for the leadership. Hosea's allusions to the exodus from Egypt (2:15; 7:11; 8:13; 9:3; 11:1, 5; 12:9, 13; 13:4) and a handful of references to divine laws (4:6; 8:1, 12) imagine the encounter between Israel and the Lord at Horeb/Sinai as a loyalty oath between sovereign Lord and subordinate Israel. As Israel's divine king, the Lord demands absolute loyalty from a devoted and unwavering people. Israel's failure to follow through on this pledge – placing its trust in other gods and in other human powers – triggers the wrath of a betrayed sovereign, articulated with reference to and worked out by the hand of current military powers.

In a more contemporary context, we might consider the ways in which our failures to live according to the Lord's requirements – to do justice, to love mercy and to walk humbly with God, as Hosea's slightly younger contemporary Micah was to put it – work themselves out in situations of pain and suffering in our lives, in the lives of those around us and in the lives of those over whom we exert authority or a special duty of care. Though we call them by other names – power, sex and money, to name a few – rather than Baal or Asherah, the modern world offers just as many opportunities for us to divert our loyalties from God.

1 Israel's sin and captivity

Hosea 10

Hosea 10 begins with a condemnation of Israel's ingratitude. Rather than becoming good stewards of the blessings heaped upon them by the Lord, Israel has wasted its resources worshipping false gods. They have placed their trust in material things, whose unreliability as a foundation for life will be revealed by their ready collapse at the hand of the Lord. Israel's orientation toward the wrong ends is revealed further in their carelessness in their relationships. They do not keep their word. Because they renege on their promises and oaths, the networks of mutual trust that hold society together are beginning to collapse, with accusations and indictments flying around like birds of prey on the hunt.

Yet still Israel misunderstands its calamities, thinking that the cause of its distress stems from its failure to worship its other gods assiduously enough. Hosea mocks the people for their foolishness; their idols are mere objects, powerless to prevent their own deportation to foreign lands. Two centuries later and already in a foreign land himself, Isaiah makes similar mockery of those who worship the Babylonian gods, who cannot bear the burdens of their people but must themselves be borne on the people's backs (Isaiah 46). Again, we see signs that Hosea knows about Assyrian modes of conquest: because idols were perceived as representing a deity's presence, the Assyrians made a habit of 'godnapping' these statues from conquered territories, transporting them back to Mesopotamia and holding them hostage to ensure the compliance of their worshippers. Here, the Lord hopes that the humiliation of Israel's idols will prompt Israel to realise their impotence, to reconsider their allegiances and to recognise the Lord as their one true God.

Verses 11 and following emphasise that God has delayed judgement to this point but can hold out no longer. The rapid shifts in terminology for the people – Ephraim, Judah, Jacob, Israel – reflects the later conclusion that the people have, in all their different manifestations over the course of their history, been persistently recalcitrant and stubborn in their refusals to recognise the Lord. The social consequences of this failure are brought to the fore in the chapter's final verses: because they have failed to walk in the ways of their God, the people have neglected the Lord's summons to justice and righteousness, sowing wickedness and injustice instead. It is no surprise that society is on the brink of collapse.

2 God's compassion despite Israel's ingratitude

Hosea 11:1—12:1

The prophets often remind Israel of its past history with the Lord in their attempts to summon it back to faithfulness (e.g. Jeremiah 2—3; Ezekiel 16; 20; 23). Thus chapter 11 begins with the recollection of God's past dealings with Israel. Unlike Jeremiah 2—3, which sees these early years as a sort of honeymoon period, Hosea hints at Israel's struggles to commit to the Lord already from the relationship's earliest stages in Egypt. Later, Ezekiel will take this idea to its extreme, characterising Israel's relationship with the Lord as a disaster from the start (Ezekiel 20). Israel, it seems, has always been commitment-phobic, stumbling again and again toward the temptations posed by less demanding deities and away from the Lord. Israel has directed its love towards lifeless idols, blind to the Lord's love for his people.

The image of the Lord in verses 1–4 is striking, describing Israel as God's own child and God as intensely parental, perhaps even specifically maternal. Though language describing God like a woman is not very common in the biblical texts, it does appear intermittently, and the biblical authors do not seem afraid to use it. Isaiah, for example, imagines God as a woman in labour (Isaiah 21:3; 42:14). The metaphor of God as our parent appears already in Genesis 1, evoked by our description as being made in God's image (Genesis 1:26–27; compare Genesis 5:1–3). Israel, however, has rejected its begetter. It has turned away from God, thinking to find other sustenance; instead it will find itself turned towards foreign nations and made to march out into exile.

The reference to the Most High to which the people call, in error (v. 7), is perhaps a reference to a title for the Canaanite high god El, who, like Baal, was a rival for the people's attentions. In other texts, the title 'Most High' is taken over by the Lord (Deuteronomy 32:8; 2 Samuel 22:14; Psalm 7:17; 9:2; 18:13; 21:7, etc.; Daniel 4). The Lord's distress at the situation is expressed in verse 8; like a parent obliged to discipline a beloved child, the Lord hates to inflict suffering on Israel. The allusions to Admah and Zeboiim are a rarer version of allusions to Sodom and Gomorrah, with which they were destroyed

(Deuteronomy 29:23). Verses 9–11 look forward to a future in which judgement has come and gone, the Lord's anger is spent and the Israelites will be welcomed home once more. Verse 11 looks back from a different perspective, after Israel's deportation, to claim that those still left in Judah are there because they have been faithful and not displeased the Lord.

3 The long history of rebellion

Hosea 12:2–14

Judah is now brought into the dock alongside Israel, although the indictment of Israel is lodged primarily against Israel's alter ego, Jacob. This is the longest and most detailed allusion to the traditions about Jacob to appear in the entire Bible, save for the more systematic presentation of his various shenanigans in Genesis (Jacob is notoriously a trickster – wheeling and dealing with his uncle and stealing blessings from his brother). Hosea pays special attention to two episodes that highlight Jacob's stubbornness: his antenatal struggles with his brother Esau, which were taken to symbolise what would become a long-running and sibling-like rivalry between Israel and Edom (Genesis 25), and Jacob's wrestling match with God by the river Jabbok, at the place he then named Peniel (Genesis 32).

The latter is an intriguing allusion, for it was precisely because Jacob struggled with God, insisting on a blessing, that he gained his new name, Israel. Indeed, the name Israel specifically highlights this propensity to struggle with God. Although the primary focus in Hosea is on Israel's struggles against God, the Bible is full of stories of faithful individuals who struggled with God in their belief – Jeremiah and Job, for example. Both of these fought with God especially over their frustration at God's apparent abandonment of the ways of righteousness and of justice; in the end, both were themselves found righteous in their struggles, despite their inability to perceive the ultimate ways of God. Even Jesus, during his last night with the disciples on the Mount of Olives, struggled with God over his future.

The trouble with Israel, says Hosea, is that its recent struggles with God have not been in pursuit of love and justice. Rather, the people of Israel have rejected God's demand that they walk with integrity and honesty, preferring to fiddle the accounts to cheat others and enrich themselves. The warning that through the prophets the Lord will bring destruction echoes instructions later given to Ezekiel and to Jeremiah, which presume that one of the functions of a prophet is to warn the people of their wayward tendencies and attempt to coax them back into the fold. If the people refuse to listen they are justly condemned, for they have been given the opportunity to change their ways. Through the prophets' unheeded warnings, then, come destruction.

4 Relentless judgement on Israel

Hosea 13

Hosea returns here to Israel's errant pursuit of Baal in lieu of the Lord. This worship of Baal is materially focused on Baal's representation as a bull-calf, cast in metal, but the offence is far more grievous than merely expressing a predilection for shiny objects. Rather, Israel's obsession with Baal has left it with no interest in the Lord. The heavy weight of Baal's cast silver bull is illusory, says Hosea; this god is as ephemeral as the mist, incapable of going the distance. This is the same god that chapter 10 warned would be carried off into exile, powerless even to defend itself.

This contrasts mightily with the steadfastness of the Lord. Israel's God has persisted with and provided for the people from the earliest days of their relationship, from their exodus in power from Egypt and the perils of their sojourn in the wilderness. Israel has shamefully forgotten this rock of its salvation, ignoring the real strength of the Lord in favour of the false strength of other gods. The Lord's punishment of Israel is, in part, an attempt to regain the people's attention, proving that it is really the Lord who exerts the power of life and death over the creatures of the earth. Verses 7–8 do this with vivid images of God as a wild beast of prey, focused so unwaveringly upon Israel that it is as though he is stalking them (compare Amos 1:2; 3:4–5, 8; 5:18–20).

That the Lord will be 'like a bear robbed of her cubs' (v. 8) evokes again the Lord's parental grief at being deprived of his people, even if their estrangement is a result of the people's own rebellion. Israel is described as a stubborn child – so stubborn that he refuses to be born, even though this will surely consign him to Sheol. This power of death threatens to overcome the people because of their apostasy; thus is the severity of Israel's turn away from the Lord. The shocking imagery of the final verse underscores the gravity and long-lasting consequences of Israel's rebelliousness. Indeed, throughout the latter half of the chapter, Hosea's rhetoric consistently affirms that Israel's religious failings are so grave as to be a matter of life and death. Israel's present stubbornness – its refusal to respond to the call of the Lord and come forth into life – has doomed the future – represented by the children and pregnant women of verse 16 – to death.

5 A plea for repentance

Hosea 14:1–3

After the climactic pronouncement on Israel's death-dealing ways, Hosea makes one final attempt to persuade his audience to repent. Israel is cast once more as an unlearnt child, stumbling in foolish things. Its fate, however, is not utterly sealed; there is still the possibility of return to the Lord.

This plea for Israel to return to its God is a recurring motif throughout the prophetic texts. It is perhaps otherwise most clearly pronounced by the prophet Jeremiah, whose opening chapters echo again and again with cries of 'Repent!', 'Return!' and 'Turn back!', in his desperate efforts to turn the Israelites away from the way of death and back towards the way of the Lord, the source of life (Jeremiah 2—6). What is required is simple: Israel's acknowledgement of its past sin and its recognition that the Lord alone is able to absolve it; a commitment to the pursuit of the good, accompanied by the orientation of all its being towards the Lord in praise; the rejection of the claims of mere mortal authorities to the power of salvation; and the rejection of material goods as unworthy of worship.

The final line of verse 3 presents the alternatives before Israel in stark terms. Without the Lord, Israel is an orphan, exposed and vulnerable, preyed upon by all who find him. The Lord offers the shelter of a beloved parent, opening his arms to the lost and bereaved and turning them once again towards the right path.

6 Assurance of forgiveness

Hosea 14:4–9

The richness of Israel's relationship with the Lord, should Israel take up this summons to return, is described using extended arboreal metaphors, first describing Israel and then the Lord as well-rooted trees. This promise of well-being is couched in the first-person speech of the Lord, emphasising that it is God himself who will care for Israel. The imagery may be intended to evoke the floral abundance of the primordial garden, in which God provided for all the humans' needs.

It is also reminiscent of the extended garden imagery of the Song of Solomon, in which the lovers' care for each other is described as the luxuriant abundance of a well-tended garden, and thus brings us full circle to the sexual metaphors of the opening chapters, albeit here in a somewhat more muted form. Indeed, though chapters 1—3 also speak of the unconditionality of the Lord's love for Israel, there the relationship is marred by Israel's waywardness and God's anger. Here, both are gone; Israel has returned to the Lord and the Lord loves Israel freely (v. 4). The lovers are at peace in themselves and with each other. We recall again that this is a future possible only through divine grace.

There is a wordplay on 'Ephraim' in the beginning and end of the passage: 'I will heal' (*erpa*) in verse 4 and the word translated by NRSV as 'your faithfulness' in verse 8, which in Hebrew is 'your fruit' (*peryeka*). Ephraim will be healed by the Lord and blessed with abundance. Although it is obscured by the English, verse 7 also has a play on the verbs for 'to return' (*šwb*) and 'to dwell' (*yšb*), promising that those who return to the Lord will dwell in his protection.

The exact meaning of the question in verse 8 is uncertain, but it seems to reflect the book's keen insistence on the antithesis between Israel's worship of the Lord and Israel's worship of idols of various kinds. The latter are at last abandoned; Israel/Ephraim will recognise the Lord as the one God able to respond to Israel's entreaties and as the true source of divine care and protection. Neither material distractions nor the temptation of the gods they represent will any longer come between Israel and its Lord.

The final verse characterises idolatry as foolishness and advocates the wise discernment of the ways of the Lord. In its piety, it perhaps glosses over how difficult such discernment can be – one need only look back at

24–30 June

the beginning of the chapter to recall Israel's propensity to stumble in its attempts to walk in the ways of the Lord. Proper discernment of the ways of God is an ideal towards which we strive, albeit one with regard to which we frequently fall short.

Guidelines

Hosea summons us to examine where we place our time and our trust. Although Hosea's focus is on the other gods that claim Israel's attention and divert it from its devotion to the Lord, his warnings of the futility and, indeed, the destructiveness of distractions from God are relevant more generally. Whether by our quests for professional success, our attempts to assuage consuming anxieties about our reputations and legacy, or our pursuit of wealth, prestige and other forms of power, we are surrounded by internal and external pressures to perform, to achieve, to maintain illusions of perfection.

All these demands clamour for our finite supply of energy and attention, drawing us away from God. Like the ancient Israelites, we delude ourselves about the source of our being and purpose. We believe we will succeed if we make the right supplication to the right boss at the right time. We will be blessed with financial and material abundance through offerings to stock markets and savings accounts. We divine our children's futures from Ofsted reports. Our faith in these things is misplaced. As Hosea implores us: these things will not save us (14:3).

Fortunately for us, the Lord awaits our return, uniquely able to forget the sins of our past and desirous of beginning with us anew. The marital metaphor with which Hosea began, in pain and in suffering for all parties, comes finally into its fullest and most potent expression at the end: as an image of the intensity of God's desire for us and of the overwhelming and passionate desire we should have for God in return. Unlike the ephemeral diversions of material things, the love of the Lord is steadfast and resolute.

FURTHER READING

Gerlinde Baumann, tr. Linda M. Maloney, *Love and Violence: Marriage as a metaphor for the relationship between YHWH and Israel in the prophetic books* (Liturgical Press, 2003).

J. Andrew Dearman, *The Book of Hosea (New International Commentary on the Old Testament)* (Eerdmans, 2010).

Francis Landy, *Hosea (Readings: A new biblical commentary)*, 2nd ed. (Sheffield Phoenix, 2011).

James Limburg, *Hosea – Micah (Interpretation: A Bible commentary for teaching and preaching)* (Westminster John Knox, 2011).

Carol A. Newsom, Jacqueline E. Lapsley and Sharon H. Ringe, *Women's Bible Commentary*, 3rd ed., revised and updated (Westminster John Knox, 2012).

Shalom: God's manifesto

Andrew Francis

'Shalom' is a Hebrew word that recurs throughout the Bible. Depending upon its context, it has different meanings with no single, direct English translation. Shalom was also a dominant mark and motif of the words, works and ways of the earthly Jesus. Therefore, in our following after Jesus, shalom must be central to our discipleship's expression.

As a writer, I keep rediscovering how many leading theologians, with different perspectives and trajectories, have written about shalom as part of their wider thesis for mission and discipleship. Some are named within our reflections, but you may well know others too. Shalom is so vital to our 'life in God' that it simply cannot be ignored, wherever we come from – spiritually and theologically.

The word 'shalom', with its Arabic derivative *salaam*, is important to all three Abrahamic faiths of Judaism, Christianity and Islam. Although Jerusalem was named originally after a Canaanite deity, modern Jewish etymology ascribes the city as 'house of shalom' or 'place of peace', with parallel Arabic/Palestinian understandings using *salaam*. Like Jerusalem the city, shalom creates an uneasy tension for its claimed adherents, and to misunderstand either throws life into imbalance. Shalom has political and theological significance.

As we consider shalom, I invite you to use the suggested Bible reading to act as a mirror to help you reflect upon how the Bible exemplifies God's shalom. In reflecting about shalom, we realise that it is a cloth woven through the threads of the Christian Bible, as the various cross-references reveal. The biblical passage set for each day is an important source for developing our understanding of shalom. So, while the notes do not always 'exegete' the passage, the biblical material is foundational for what follows. Hence, I encourage you to read this and reflect on it carefully.

Unless otherwise stated, Bible quotations are from the New Revised Standard Version (Anglicised).

1 Much more than peace

Isaiah 65:17–25

Too often, shalom is mistranslated as simply meaning 'peace'. This is because the Greek word *eirene*, meaning 'peace', has often replaced the Hebrew word shalom in later Greek versions of the Bible. When that *eirene* is further translated into the Latin word *pax* (which also means 'peace') or one of its derivatives, en route into modern-language translation, we can begin to understand how the modern Christian church so often belittles shalom as simply peace – in the sense of an absence of military conflict.

Previously, I have written, 'In the Hebrew sense of God's shalom, peace is a bigger concept. It is a world in which grace and generosity, non-violence, conflict mediation and assertive meekness are the dominant model of human character in its dealings with others' (*Shalom: The Jesus manifesto*, 2016). This is the peace that we see brought forward in the life and ministry of Jesus.

One example of this is in Jesus' dealing with both the woman caught in adultery and the crowd desirous of stoning her, in John 8. Jesus intervenes non-violently in the conflict, assertively stating, 'Let anyone among you who is without sin be the first to throw a stone at her' (v. 7), causing the mob to melt away. When Jesus is left with only the woman, they recognise a 'peace' has been restored as Jesus instructs her, 'Go your way, and from now on do not sin again' (v. 11). Jesus is providing us with a gracious model of non-violent peacemaking.

Such shalom brings risk, as Jesus invites his followers 'to turn the other [cheek]' (Matthew 5:39). We risk injury, even death, to share in God's shalom. We have to believe a greater peace is possible, when evil or human conflict become overwhelming. Just think of God's picture of shalom in the visionary imagery of Isaiah 65, when the lion will lie down with the lamb. God's shalom is so overwhelmingly proclaiming a new world order of peace.

That does not mean that hurt is not part of the human journey. That peaceable, assertive meekness is revealed in Jesus' response to Pilate's question 'Are you the King of the Jews?' (Mark 15:2) and Jesus' submission to death upon the cross so that God's shalom for all creation will ultimately prevail.

2 Shalom means justice

One of my favourite passages from the Hebrew testament is the courtroom scene from Micah. The prophet describes how the world's age-old mountains witness to the temporal and abusive actions of humanity. Finally, the prophet reminds us what the Lord does require: to 'act justly, love mercy and walk humbly with and before God' (v. 8, my translation). For Christians, Jesus exemplifies such discipleship.

One central insight of the Bible is that God is the God of justice. God condemns and corrects injustice. Jesus carries that forward throughout his ministry, inviting those who receive forgiveness to 'mend their ways', and even offer reparation. Consider the Zacchaeus episode (Luke 19:1–10) and how this repentant tax collector repays fourfold those whom he has cheated.

God's intentions for shalom-justice are not easy. Israel's horrible history of murder, duplicity, genocide, usury, slavery and abuse of women (all as recorded in that Hebrew testament) can be seen in the actions of despots and nations over the last two millennia and into today's world. Is it any wonder that another prophet, Amos, used a plumb line to declare whether Israel measured up to God's intention (Amos 7:7)? It leaves us to ask how well both the church and our individual lives measure up to God's intention.

The work of black, 'green', feminist and liberation theologians together helps us question how we handle God's world with (in)justice as we look at the treatment of other races, women, the poor, etc. – and creation itself. Justice means being good stewards of God's creation. Increasingly, I find that I cannot teach about the 'household of God' (Greek *oikos*) without drawing in a theology of shalom.

That same shalom cannot relegate others to deprivation, ill treatment or abuse. But these are marks of the world which invade virtually every news bulletin. The world does not acknowledge shalom. Only those who know their 'life in God' can begin to understand, accept and then begin to live by shalom. History is dominated by injustice and greed. God's shalom is countercultural, calling us to lay down our selfish desires for power and wealth and to 'act justly, love mercy and walk humbly with God', who revealed his shalom in the life, ministry, unjust death and resurrection of Jesus.

3 Shalom equals well-being for all

John 10:7–16

The flipside of the coin of justice is well-being. Jesus said, 'I came that they may have life, and have it abundantly' (v. 10). In the Jesus-shaped community, there can be no half-measures for some of our sisters and brothers. God's intention is that there be no second-class citizens.

How we define well-being will somewhat depend upon where we live in God's world. It will mean that people do not go hungry or thirsty or without warm, secure shelter. Friends in Orkney and others such as rural African aid workers have different healthcare expectations to those in suburban Birmingham. Well-being may have its geographical nuances but its divine intention is obvious.

What it will mean for us all, with education and influence, is that we work to enable the world to be more equal and remove the causes of deprivation. We should all be rebuked by eco-feminist theologian Dorothee Sölle's remark, 'To feed the hungry means to do away with militarism' (*Theology for Sceptics*, 1995, p. 92). The biblical teaching of Proverbs (25:21) is irenic, as it exhorts the Jews to feed and water those whom they might regard as enemies. In a world of inequalities and wars over resources, we have to learn to share the 'bread' we have if there is to be well-being for all.

The Swedish word *lagom* literally means 'team round' but colloquially means 'not too little, not too much'. *Lagom* is a watchword (and plumb line!) for Swedish society. Effectively, it means not taking too much, whether at the mealtable with friends or neighbours, or in the size of our homes and cars, or simply in our share of the world's resources. *Lagom* is shalom in action. It is the discipleship challenge of the interplay between *lagom* and shalom that has led my partner and I to downsize our housing and resource needs.

Life in all its fullness has practical, everyday implications for us all. It is why so many of us campaigned against apartheid and other inequalities, write letters for Amnesty International, support Oxfam or Water Aid, or work in our local foodbank. Shalom should be who and what we are. God's intention for well-being must become the fabric of our daily lives. Shalom demands well-being for all.

4 The covenant and community of shalom

The biblical theologian Walter Brueggemann wrote, 'The vision of wholeness, which is the supreme will of the biblical God, is the outgrowth of a covenant of shalom (Ezekiel 34:25), in which persons are bound not only to God but to one another in a caring, sharing, rejoicing community with none to make them afraid' (*Living Toward a Vision*, 2nd edition, 1982, p. 17). What a single-sentence manifesto for the Jesus community!

The concept of 'covenant' is rooted deep within the Hebrew testament and people. It is the declaration of a known agreement, which creates an ongoing relationship. In human terms, we often use marriage as an example of a covenant. In Jeremiah (31:31–33), we hear God declare, 'I will be their God and they shall be my people,' speaking of the ongoing but preexisting covenant. No wonder Israel means 'chosen people': those who wrestle with God's intentions. Choice is an essential element in the participation within both God's covenant and God's shalom: for rich westerners, we should choose to step back from our over-consumption of the world's finite resources.

There is mutuality in the community of shalom. Recall how Jesus asks the Samaritan woman for a drink (John 4:4–15), creating a mutuality as he reaches out across the racial and gender divides. Again, Jesus tempers his earthly frustration with the Canaanite woman into mutuality when she challenges him (Matthew 15:21–28), acknowledging her faith. Consider the early church: in Acts, we read how they shared 'all things in common' daily (2:43–47), and how human divisions were overcome, as seen in today's passage and in Philemon.

Lesslie Newbigin repeatedly taught that the earthly Jesus left a community of faith not a book of instructions. That community is empowered by the Spirit to be covenantally one, enabling an equality within mutual service to each other, the world's people and the world with all its resources. It was the patient fermenting of such evident mutuality within the early church which enabled the nascent Christian community to grow.

During my lifetime, I have been blessed to stay in radical households, such as those of the Catholic Worker Movement and the Jesus Army, and in more widespread 'common purse' communities, such as Bruderhof and Emmaus, experiencing in each their covenant and community of shalom. They act as some contemporary plumb lines of God's possibilities.

5 Shalom proclaims a bigger vision

Revelation 21:22—22:6

It is both logical and obvious that if we accept shalom's manifesto, as revealed in the Bible's pages and God's manifestation in Jesus, as meaning well-being for all, it will call us to a bigger vision for God's world.

A couple of years ago, my book *OIKOS: God's big word for a small planet* (2017) was published as a theology of economy, ecology and ecumeny. Its purpose was to demonstrate the interrelationship between the world's economic trajectory, the deepening ecological crises and our failure to build stronger human community. It utilised the biblical concept behind the Greek word *oikos*, which means 'house' or 'household', to demonstrate why we must question the negatives and how we must build the positives if God's new world order of shalom is to be realised. We need bigger vision.

Within our learning as Christians, we have to grow continually in our understanding of the new day which God in Christ is bringing. It will mean redemption for all creation, when all is made well – this is the ultimate shalom. Personally, I wrestle with the differing pictures of that end time in Revelation; I find the final vision of the heavenly city in today's passage more helpful than those of the different judgements (14:14–20 or 16:1–21). Shalom's vision is of a time that is coming when God will preside over only well-being and blessing.

But in the interim, we live with the uneasy tensions of a world with both haves and have-nots. We live in a world where greed and aspiration are valued more than servanthood and sharing. We need the encouragement and nurture of God's new community to live counterculturally; whether it is in home-based prayer group or grand cathedral worship, we need to share in those moments where we catch the vision of all the saints – both on earth and in heaven.

In both those multi-voiced worship settings, everyone is vital to its well-being: where would we be without our prayer partners or what would cathedral worship be like without its choirs, its vergers and readers, its congregation and celebrants? Shalom's vision values everyone – and we must learn to do the same.

6 Shalom brings salvation

Shalom is a central, practical tenet of *missio Dei* – God's mission to the world. If we are God's people, we are part of that mission. As we are made in God's image (Genesis 1:26–27), we can choose to accept the divine intention for our lives and live out shalom as exemplarily shown in Jesus' words, works and ways – or not, to our peril.

Metanoia is the Greek word for 'conversion'; literally, it means 'turning around'. That is what many must do as the gospel/good news of God's shalom impacts their lives. They, and we, are called away from the life of self and greed, which denies others an equal opportunity to share God's life and fullness in this world – and the next.

Within the classic four credal notes of the church, there is an interrelationship (echoing that of the Trinity) in which one cannot exist without the others. For the church to be truly missional, or apostolic, in its work in the world, it is called to be 'one' and 'holy' and 'catholic', therefore open to all, and so on. The salvation of the world is not just about individual souls or the stewardship of creation but the subsumation of God's church within the shalom of *missio Dei*.

We need to nurture our friends, family and neighbours in the discussion of shalom's vision. Among non-believers, I find that easiest around the meal table. Is it easier to say 'Come for a meal' or 'Come to church on Sunday'? God calls us to build shalom-based relationships and we see that echoed in Jesus' 'eat, pray, tell' instructions as he sends his disciples out in pairs (Matthew 10:5–15; Luke 9:1–6). As the Middle Eastern proverb says, 'The hand of friendship is the root of hospitality.' Sharing food, faith and friendship are central to shalom-based mission.

Britain's increasing secularisation means that we have to find 'fresh wineskins' (Matthew 9:17) as we share the *missio Dei*. The church's history of violence and planetary abuse tells us why the 'reign of God' and shalom can never be fully portrayed within the church. It is in the turning around and breaking out into new ways of being God's people in the world that will enable others to share 'life in all its fullness' of God's salvation and all-embracing shalom.

Guidelines

Understanding shalom in theory is akin to building up a three-dimensional jigsaw of understanding. It becomes far more apparent if we begin to practise shalom as a central part of discipleship each and every day – we need look no further than Jesus for the role model. But, after this week together, why not ask yourself afresh:

- Why is shalom so much part of Jesus' words, works and ways?

- How much is shalom who we are as God's people?

- In what ways is your lifestyle challenged to embrace deeper shalom?

- Among which groups of people (communities?) have you most experienced the lifestyle of shalom?

- If you had only five minutes, what part of God's shalom vision would you share with a non-believing friend?

… then take a few months, if not a lifetime, to make your answers come alive. But in that dynamic interim, here is a prayer for the journey:

Gracious God,
whose intention in creation is that all may share
in your peace, provision and plenty,
teach us to live in communities and homes of shalom,
that others may see your life, love and goodness,
as we follow in the words, works and ways of Jesus,
whose Spirit empowers our very being.
Amen

FURTHER READING

Walter Brueggemann, *Living Toward a Vision: Biblical reflections on shalom* (UCP, 1982).

Andrew Francis, *Eat, Pray, Tell: A relational approach to 21st-century mission* (BRF, 2018).

Andrew Francis, *OIKOS: God's big word for a small planet* (Cascade, 2017).

Andrew Francis, *Shalom: The Jesus manifesto* (Paternoster, 2016).

Perry B. Yoder, *Shalom: The Bible's word for salvation, justice and peace* (Faith and Life Press, 1976).

Luke 19:1—22:2

Steve Walton

Luke's story is drawing towards its climax in Jerusalem. Jesus has been on the road to the city for a long while (since 9:51) and he finally approaches and enters Jerusalem. Here, the challenges he faces will intensify in response to his greater clarity over who he is as Israel's king and Lord. He will enter and repossess the temple, both negatively, by throwing out the traders, and positively, by teaching there regularly.

His teaching will continue to clarify and state what he is about and what he is not about. His calling is to seek and save lost people, rather than to pander to 'religious' people's cultural mores. This means he will face hostility from the Jewish leaders who recognise his claim to be Israel's king and reject it – throughout this section, we shall see the plot to get rid of Jesus escalate.

Jesus told his disciples in advance where events were leading, even though they didn't understand (18:31–34). When he sees tensions developing, there are some things he needs his disciples to know before he is arrested, including how to live without him during periods of suffering and persecution. He needs them to know that life as his followers will not be a smooth ride – rather the opposite – but that he will stand with them and equip them, even though he may be physically absent.

Because the focus of God's people will be on Jesus in the future, the Jewish temple in Jerusalem has had its day. It has been a valuable symbol of God's presence among his people, but his people – especially their leaders – have failed to see that Jesus is now going to be the route to God, not this complex of buildings, however impressive. Jesus' startling teaching about the temple will precipitate the final crisis which leads to his death.

Unless otherwise stated, Bible quotations are from the New Revised Standard Version (Anglicised).

1 I want you to get right out of your tree!

Luke 19:1–10

Jesus' long journey to Jerusalem from the north is nearing its end: he is in Jericho, about 22 km (14 miles) from Jerusalem (v. 1). We have seen him heal a blind beggar on the edge of Jericho (18:35–43); now, he engages with a wealthy man, Zacchaeus – Luke again 'pairs' contrasting characters in adjacent stories (the chapter division is unhelpful here).

Zacchaeus' role as a chief tax collector (v. 2) would fit in the well-to-do society of Jericho, an ancient city with a temperate climate, which made it a popular place for well-off people to have second homes; the city may have been headquarters for his role, overseeing tax collection for a region. However, Zacchaeus would not have been popular among his fellow Jews, for the tax collectors collaborated with the Roman oppressors. They were notorious for abusing their ability to charge over the odds in taxes, and then pocket the surplus.

Both his unpopularity and his size meant Zacchaeus had to find a way to see Jesus, and he climbed a fig-mulberry tree (v. 4; not like a 'sycamore', which is part of the maple family). These trees grow to 18 metres (60 feet) tall, and have low, thick branches, which makes them easy to climb, and large leaves, which makes it easy not to be seen if you have climbed one. From this vantage point, Zacchaeus could see, but not easily be seen.

What a shock it must have been, then, when Jesus not only noticed Zacchaeus, but addressed him by name and invited himself to Zacchaeus' house (v. 5)! Zacchaeus responded with enthusiasm (v. 6), by contrast with the murmuring of others (v. 7) – an echo of earlier criticism of Jesus' eating with tax collectors and sinners (15:1–2). In Luke 15, we learned through three parables about Jesus' seeking of lost people, as we do here (v. 10). Now we learn more, that truly meeting Jesus is transformative (v. 8): Zacchaeus responds by giving a huge amount of his wealth away – 50% to the poor – and repaying four times over anything he has cheated, which would make quite a hole in the remaining 50%!

This transformation shows that 'salvation' has come to Zacchaeus' house (v. 9) – Luke does not explicitly *tell* us that Zacchaeus repented, but he does *show* it by the change to Zacchaeus' lifestyle and attitudes.

2 A double parable (1)

Jesus tells a double parable in response to the idea that his talk of God's kingdom meant that it was about to appear (v. 11; see also 17:20–21). Jesus speaks with a general audience, including some opponents (19:7).

The outer parable (vv. 12, 14, 27) reflects events in Judea after Herod the Great's death (4BC). Because power lay with the emperor, Herod's sons Archelaus and Antipas went to Rome to ask to be made king following their father. However, the Jewish leaders sent a delegation to oppose Archelaus, and the brothers were allowed to rule as 'ethnarch' and 'tetrach' (respectively), rather than king. Ten years later, a further Judean delegation successfully asked for Archelaus' removal.

This parable portrays Jesus as a nobleman going away to be given a kingship. There is no indication how long or short a time he is away, and so the parable provides no timetable for Jesus' return as king. However, even though Jesus is presently opposed (see 19:7), he will return as king: his kingly rule is real, but not yet fully seen. This parable poses a stark choice: whose side are the audience on, for that will be the side they are on at the last day when they answer to King Jesus.

The inner parable (vv. 13, 15–26) focuses on the king-to-be's slaves in the time before he returns as king. By contrast with Matthew's parable of the talents (Matthew 25:14–30), all ten slaves are given the same relatively small amount, a mina (v. 13; NRSV 'pound' – roughly three months' wages for a labourer), and this parable picks out just three of them. Matthew's parable is located after Jesus arrives in Jerusalem, whereas Luke's is in Jericho (9:1, 11). They look like two parables sharing a similar outline but making different (although related) points.

The small amount of money the slaves are given is a test of their trustworthiness (v. 17) in their master's absence, and their actions inform him whether he can trust them with greater responsibilities. The two productive slaves receive a reward completely out of proportion to their work – responsibility for cities, rather than money (vv. 17, 19). The master is evidently now a king, for he has responsibility for cities to hand out. To serve Jesus faithfully results in greater responsibility, according to a person's ability and execution of the tasks God gives them.

3 A double parable (2)

In the latter part of this double parable (see notes on 19:11–19), Jesus continues to address two kinds of people: first, those who claim to be his followers (vv. 20–26) and then those who presently oppose him (v. 27).

The unproductive slave hid his money (v. 20) rather than placing it with the untrustworthy banks common in the ancient world – you might well lose your money rather than gain interest. Our reaction to the way the returned king treats him is that it seems unfair, disproportionate for a small amount and unworthy of Jesus. However, not every detail of a parable corresponds to what God is like and how God acts. The king's high-handed actions against this slave would have been common – even expected – from a ruler in the ancient world.

In the parable of the unjust judge (18:1–8), the judge is not meant to correspond to God at every point – the force of that parable is to call people to persist in prayer (18:1). Likewise, here Jesus is not 'a harsh man' (vv. 21–22), holding outrageous expectations of his servants. This part of the inner parable is designed to cause professing disciples of Jesus to reflect and act concerning what we are doing – and will do – with the shared responsibilities which God gives to us all (for all the slaves here receive the same). The parable doesn't spell out what those 'minas' are, and that suggests they represent the tasks and responsibilities which the whole believing community shares, given by Jesus, including holiness, discipleship, mission and evangelism, social engagement, and so on.

What of the citizens who opposed the king (v. 27), perhaps because they didn't expect him to be made king? The parable starkly portrays their rejection by the king: they are to be killed in front of him. This shocking picture does not stand alone in Luke: judgement and division have been portrayed in similarly stark terms in other parables (e.g. 12:36–46; 16:1–9; 18:1–8). Jesus' purpose here is to show people in picture, even cartoon, form the choice they now face – the enemy who chooses to oppose the king is treated far more severely than the unproductive slave. This part of the story calls for serious reflection by its hearers: are they out or in with Jesus?

4 Here comes the king!

Luke 19:28–38

This incident is often called Jesus' 'triumphal entry' into Jerusalem, and some say that the people of Jerusalem acclaim him here, only to turn against him and call for him to be crucified days later. In fact, neither is true. First, Jesus does not enter Jerusalem until 19:45 – this incident happens on the way to Jerusalem, as Jesus and his disciples come over the hill at Bethphage and get their first sight of the city (v. 29).

Jesus' message, 'The Lord needs it' (v. 34), is not a claim about himself as 'Lord' – Luke is careful not to 'read back' into his gospel stories the understanding of Jesus as Lord which his second book records (Acts 2:36). Rather, his hearers and disciples would understand him as saying, '*God* needs it' – it may have been a code phrase arranged with the colt's owners and known to Jesus' friends in the village.

Jesus' action involves a remarkable claim. It was usual for Passover pilgrims to arrive in the city on foot. So Jesus' deliberate choice to travel on a colt is striking – this is the only time in Luke he does not walk – and echoes Zechariah 9:9 (NIV): 'Rejoice greatly, Daughter Zion! Shout, Daughter Jerusalem! See, your king comes to you, righteous and victorious, lowly and *riding on a donkey, on a colt, the foal of a donkey*' (my emphasis). A donkey was the animal which a civil official, such as a judge, might ride, and not a military animal – an army commander would ride a horse. Indeed, in Israel, David's successors rode to their coronation on a donkey (e.g. 1 Kings 1:32–40) – the combination of these biblical echoes identifies Jesus as Israel's king.

The disciples recognise this claim, and they – not the people of Jerusalem at large – praise God joyfully and loudly (v. 37). They recognise the claim of Jesus' symbolic action and adapt the standard pilgrim's welcome from Psalm 118:26, 'Blessed is the one who comes in the name of the Lord', by replacing 'the one' with 'the *king*' (v. 38). They also spread their cloaks on the road after the manner of those acclaiming Jehu as Israel's king (v. 36; 2 Kings 9:13). They understand, at this point, what Jesus is doing and saying through his actions.

5 Jesus responds to criticism

Luke 19:39–44

Following Jesus' symbolic riding of the colt (19:29–36), Luke records two reactions, from the disciples (19:37–38) and the Pharisees (v. 39). Like the disciples, the Pharisees recognise Jesus' claim to be Israel's king; unlike the disciples, they reject this claim. This is the last we hear of the Pharisees as a group in this gospel. Outside Jerusalem, the Pharisees are influential on the ordinary people and honoured as serious about their Judaism. They have been Jesus' main opponents in Galilee and on his travels south (e.g. 5:21, 30; 6:2, 7; 7:30, 36–50; 11:37–43, 53; 12:1; 14:1–4; 15:2; 16:14). Their power and influence in Jerusalem were weaker, for the priests and Sadducees dominated there. The opposition to Jesus from here on is focused on those Jewish leaders.

Jesus responds to the Pharisees' criticism with a three-pronged answer. First, he rejects their request to silence his disciples, and implies that they are right: even the stones on the road would cry out – and perhaps the stones which formed the temple, still under construction then (v. 40).

Second, Jesus is overcome with sadness when he recognises that the city will reject him (vv. 41–42). He lamented about the city earlier (13:34–35) and will do so again (21:5–6); these three prophecies come into clearer focus as they progress. Jerusalem fails to recognise the king who brings peace when he comes – an echo of Zechariah 9:10, which portrays the king who rides into the city on a colt as proclaiming peace to the nations. The irony is considerable, for the name 'Jerusalem' means 'foundation of peace'.

Third, Jesus declares God's coming judgement following Jerusalem's rejection of him (vv. 43–44), echoing similar warnings concerning Nebuchadnezzar's successful attack on the city in 587BC (e.g. Jeremiah 6; Isaiah 29:1–4 – in the latter, the city is called 'Ariel'). In one sense, nothing new is going on – the people reject God's purposes and find God rejects them. But, in a more important sense, something new is going on, for in rejecting Jesus, the city is rejecting 'the time of your visitation' (v. 44). Zechariah earlier announces that God has *visited* his people (Luke 1:68, my translation), and when Jesus raises the widow's son at Nain from the dead, the people say, 'God has *visited* his people' (7:16, my translation). 'Visit' is what God does for his people to save them – and that's what's being seen by the disciples and missed by the Pharisees.

6 Wrong and right use of the temple courts

It was a recent innovation to allow the sale of sacrificial animals and birds within the temple courts, rather than in the market on the nearby Mount of Olives. This took place in the temple's Court of the Gentiles, an area where non-Jews could pray. Selling sacrificial animals was necessary for the temple's daily sacrifices, and for pilgrims to offer sacrifices; but the presence of the market in *this* place prevented devout Gentiles praying there.

Jesus thus protested against the sellers – he was reclaiming the temple for its proper purpose, a place where people met with God. His explanation combines two biblical echoes. 'My house shall be called a house of prayer' (Isaiah 56:7) states the temple's role clearly – and in the context, Isaiah writes of '*foreigners* who join themselves to the Lord' (56:6, my emphasis) and specifies that the house of prayer was 'for *all peoples*' (56:7, my emphasis), signalling that Gentiles could and should pray there.

'You have made it a den of robbers' (v. 46) echoes Jeremiah's 'temple sermon', quoting Jeremiah 7:11. The prophet criticises people who complacently think they are safe from invasion because God would never allow the temple to fall. Jeremiah repeats their slogan, 'This is the temple of the Lord' (7:4), and calls these 'deceptive words' (7:8).

In Luke, Jesus had only once before visited the temple, as a boy (2:41–51), and then he called it 'my Father's house' (2:49). Now, he comes to claim the temple as his own, after the manner of Malachi's prophecy that the Lord would come to purify his temple (Malachi 3:1–4), and Zechariah's statement that there would be no traders in the Lord's house when God comes to act (Zechariah 14:21). Jesus now reclaims the temple as a place of prayer by clearing the sellers out, and then occupying it himself day by day to teach (v. 47). He comes to enable people to encounter God through his ministry and actions.

As with Jesus' previous actions, this one divides: the Jewish leaders look for a way to kill him (v. 47), but 'the people' – here, the Passover pilgrims, for he taught in the temple – could not get enough teaching from him (v. 48). The division in Israel which Simeon prophesied (Luke 2:34–35) is becoming more acute.

Guidelines

Luke 19 focuses our attention on the kingship of Jesus, proclaimed in his riding the colt and his disciples' responses (vv. 28–38). In this chapter, ways in which believers are called to respond to Jesus' kingship are highlighted.

- The outer part of the parable of the pounds/minas (vv. 12, 14, 27) challenges us to consider whether Jesus is truly our king, and how much we are looking forward to his return. The Jewish leaders of Jesus' day rejected Jesus as king, and that was to lead to their rejection by God. Those men's approach shows how easy it is for apparently 'faith-full' people to miss what God is doing uniquely and particularly in and through Jesus. Are there areas of your life, and the lives of your family and your church, where you would say 'No' to Jesus if he asked you to hand them over? Those are the areas that need attention in your conversations with God.

- The inner part of the parable of the pounds/minas (vv. 13, 15–26) portrays followers of Jesus as the king's slaves and, because each slave receives the same, invites us to reflect on what we are doing with the common things which all Christians share. How are we taking our part in sharing the gospel message with others? How are we showing the welcome and hospitality which God has given to us through Jesus? How are we using the financial resources we have – however small or great – in the service of Jesus and his gospel?

- Jesus' seeking and finding Zacchaeus (vv. 1–10) focuses our attention on Jesus' mission of seeking and saving the lost (v. 10). Zacchaeus was hated by many because of his role and his ill-gotten wealth (vv. 2, 7), and yet meeting Jesus transformed him. This gives us hope that Jesus can transform the most unlikely people, and invites us to pray – and keep praying – for such people. Who are they for you?

Christ our King, give us sensitive ears to hear your voice, tender hearts to respond in love, and ready minds, hands and feet to walk with you in service. Amen

1 The question of authority

Jesus' actions on the way to Jerusalem and in the city itself involve great claims, as we have seen in Luke 19: he is Israel's king riding on a colt (19:29–36, echoing Zechariah 9:9); he accepts the disciples' acclaim as king and rejects the Pharisees' criticism of their praise (19:37–40); he clears out the sellers from the temple's Court of the Gentiles (19:45–46) and then takes it over as his place of teaching, even though he lacks formal, authorised training (19:47). These actions acutely raise the question of Jesus' authority to act and speak in this way, and Luke 20 sees Jesus in debate and confrontation with the Jewish leaders over this issue – for they think that they are the people authorised by God to speak for God.

Jesus spoke earlier of 'the elders, chief priests, and scribes' who would reject him and cause his death (9:22), and those are the people we now find opposing Jesus (20:1). They represent the main groups within the Sanhedrin, the Jewish ruling council, and we shall meet various subgroups at key points in Jesus' debates here.

They raise their key question straight out: 'Tell us, by what authority you are doing these things?' (v. 2). At first glance, Jesus' answer looks evasive: he answers a question with another question, in rabbinic manner (vv. 3–4). Beneath his response is an implicit answer, though – that he has authority identified by John the baptiser.

To see that, look back to Luke 3. There, John's role is to prepare for Jesus by calling Israel to repentance, expressed in baptism (3:3), and Luke clarifies that John is Isaiah's 'voice… crying out in the wilderness' (3:4, quoting Isaiah 40:3–5). If that is who John is, then Jesus must be 'the Lord' for whom John prepares the way (3:4). Jesus must be the one who comes after John and baptises with the Holy Spirit and fire (3:16) – and in first-century Judaism, only the God of Israel could give the Holy Spirit in that way.

Jesus is far from evading the question, as his questioners recognise (vv. 5–6), and they duck out of answering directly because neither option is palatable (v. 7). Jesus does not need to answer directly (v. 8): his answer is clear.

2 Of vineyards and tenants

Luke 20:9–19

Jesus' parable of the vineyard is his response to the leaders' question (20:2). Addressing the people with the leaders overhearing (v. 19), Jesus underlines his claim to speak for God.

The image of Israel as a vineyard is familiar from Isaiah 5, where the prophet complains that God's people are not producing the fruit God expects. Instead of cultivated grapes which produce great wine, they allow the vineyard to go wild (Isaiah 5:2). The expected 'fruit' is social justice, seen in fair courts, equitable distribution of land and a sobriety which puts the Lord at the centre (Isaiah 5:7–13). God's response is that he will turn the vineyard into a wasteland (Isaiah 5:5–6).

Jesus utilises this image to say, similarly, that Israel will lose its privileged place as God's people. Absentee landlords were common in first-century Palestine, particularly because it takes four years for a new vineyard to produce a significant crop; a new vineyard was a long-term investment, and owners would want reliable tenants to cultivate it (Isaiah 5:1). In Jesus' story, as in Isaiah 5, God is the vineyard owner. God sends his servants – the prophets – to speak to his people, and especially their leaders (the tenants), but the leaders reject the prophets (vv. 10–12; see 11:47–51; 13:33–34).

The description 'my beloved son' (v. 13) is a precise echo of the voice from heaven at Jesus' baptism (3:22), itself an echo of Psalm 2:7. Psalm 2 is a coronation psalm for Israel's king, who is called 'my [God's] beloved son' – thus the echoes through Jesus' baptism and in this parable signal that Jesus is Israel's king, coming to represent the owner. That meant he was coming to die (vv. 14–15).

Jesus hammers home his point with a quotation from Psalm 118:22, the same psalm containing the words of acclaim used on his donkey ride (19:38; Psalm 118:25–26). Jesus is the keystone at the top of the building's corner, to be lifted into that place of significance – and he will be the cause of his rejecters being broken (v. 18). The Jewish leaders recognise the challenge and the implication, and ironically set out to enact the parable by destroying the son (v. 19).

3 Taxes!

When Margaret Thatcher introduced a poll tax in the UK, it led to riots on the streets of London. Similarly, the Roman 'head tax' imposed in Judea was deeply unpopular, although not because it was heavy – it was just one denarius, a typical day's wages for a labourer – but because it symbolised the power of Rome over the Jewish people. It was debated whether to pay this tax as a matter of religious loyalty to Judaism; the question in verses 21–22 was a live one. However, the question is disingenuous, for the questioners come from the Jewish leaders ('they' in v. 20 refers to the Jewish leaders of v. 19) and only want Jesus to say something that either incriminates him with the Romans or makes him unpopular with the Judeans.

Jesus' brilliant response works at three levels. First, by having someone produce a denarius (v. 24), he demonstrates that the questioners implicitly accept Rome's right to collect the tax – indeed, the Sanhedrin were responsible for collecting this tax on Rome's behalf! Second, Jesus' question is pointed (v. 24): in asking about the 'image' on the coin – the head of the emperor – Jesus evokes the commandment which forbids images and their worship (Exodus 20:4–5). To have images was idolatry, something only pagan Gentiles would do. Third, Jesus asks about the inscription. A denarius of this period read, 'Emperor Tiberius, son of the divine Augustus' on one side – it blasphemously claimed divine honours for both Tiberius and his father, Augustus.

This was the coin used to pay the tax, and it was deeply offensive to right-thinking Jews. And yet the Sanhedrin collected these coins for the Romans – they implicitly accepted the emperor's claims. Hence Jesus says that they can 'give *back*' to Caesar what belongs to him (v. 25, NIV – the word is forceful). Further, to accept Caesar's claim to rule the world and be worthy of worship denies the worship due Israel's God alone. The emperor has a valid and limited role, but the true ruler of the world is God, not Caesar.

Jesus is not dividing the world into two: places where Caesar rules and places where God rules; rather, he is showing the hypocrisy of his questioners and pointing them to the truth they claim, but implicitly deny by paying and collecting the tax: there is one true God and he alone is worthy of worship.

4 One bride for seven brothers: a misguided puzzle

Luke 20:27–39

Now Jesus has silenced the spies (20:26), along come the Sadducees, a powerful and wealthy group who dominate the Jewish ruling council. As often, people comfortable in this world have no concern for the world-to-come: the Sadducees hold a minority position in Judaism, that there will be no resurrection (v. 27).

In order to challenge Jesus about the resurrection, they tell a bizarre story of a woman who married seven brothers successively, and yet who had no child by any of them (vv. 28–32), and end with a question to show how ridiculous resurrection is: 'Whose wife will the woman be?' (v. 33). The story turns on the levirate law of marriage, which requires that when a married man died without fathering children, his next brother must marry and have sex with the widow, and the child born would be considered to belong to the dead man, not his younger brother (Deuteronomy 25:5–6). Thus the child would inherit what his mother's first husband had left, and that man's family name would continue. (There are two biblical examples of this: Genesis 38:6–11; Ruth 4:5–10.)

In this scenario, the Sadducees make it clear that the only ongoing life they can conceive is earthly, through children. Jesus picks apart their position with precision. First, he draws a line between this age and the age to come (vv. 34–36). In this age, the Sadducees are right: a family is perpetuated by children. However, in the age to come, childbearing is no longer necessary, since the number of God's people will be complete – and thus marriage, which Jesus assumes will normally lead to childbearing, is not necessary either.

Second, the Sadducees see resurrection to be a later development, beyond the first five books of scripture (the Pentateuch), which they saw as alone divine law, and so they rejected it. Jesus takes them to Exodus 3:6 (v. 37) to show that God's ongoing covenant with Abraham, Isaac and Jacob, to be their God, means these men must be alive as far as God is concerned (v. 38). Even if the Sadducees limit themselves to the Pentateuch, resurrection is taught there. Jesus shows that the idea of resurrection is coherent and taught by scripture – and he himself will be raised from the dead and demonstrate the life of the age to come (Luke 24).

5 Great David's greater son

Jesus has silenced everyone's questions (v. 40) and now asks his own question (v. 41), posed to the people at large, concerning the interpretation of scripture offered by the teachers of the law.

It was accepted that the Messiah, who would bring God's deliverance to Israel, would be a descendant ('son') of David (v. 41), on the basis of passages such as God's promise that there would always be someone to sit on David's throne (2 Samuel 7:12–16). Jesus puts this assumption together with another passage understood messianically, Psalm 110:1 (quoted in vv. 42–43) and poses a question.

This psalm is one of the two most widely cited in the New Testament (the other is Psalm 2), and appears to have originally been composed for a coronation or a royal festival. It begins with a prophetic voice, speaking on behalf of God ('The Lord said…', v. 42). In Jesus' day, it was understood as having been composed by David, and our Bibles reflect this in the psalm heading found in the original, 'Of David'. But, says Jesus, if David is the psalm's author, and God is 'The Lord' who speaks, who is the 'my Lord' to whom God speaks? It cannot be David, since he is writing the psalm. It must refer to Israel's king, the Messiah – and that means the Messiah is greater than David, for David calls him, 'my *Lord*'.

Luke makes Jesus' descent from David clear a number of times (e.g. 1:27, 32, 69; 2:4; 3:31; 18:38–39), and we recently read of Jesus as 'king' (19:38) and saw his actions and teaching as messianic claims. But here, Jesus is going beyond what could be claimed for a human messiah, and the early Christians recognised this in their interpretations of Psalm 110:1.

At Pentecost, Peter cites this verse to show that Jesus is greater than David, since Jesus is exalted to heaven and sits in the position of honour and power at God's right side – something David never did (Acts 2:34). Peter tells the Sanhedrin that Jesus is exalted to God's right side, and therefore can offer forgiveness (Acts 5:30–31). Paul portrays Jesus sitting at God's right side, and thus believers are secure; in that place, Jesus speaks to God on our behalf (Romans 8:34). These implications flow from Jesus himself appropriating the psalm and believers later reflecting on its huge implications for Jesus' own sharing in God's identity.

6 Taking and giving

There were 13 large chests in the temple's Court of the Women and six were designated for 'freewill offerings'. They were trumpet-shaped, with the narrow part at the top to prevent theft. When pilgrims came to the temple, they would contribute to the costs of its running here. Giving was not a private, hidden activity: everyone knew *who* gave – from the noise made by the coins (which may lie behind the reference to 'trumpets' in relation to giving, Matthew 6:2) – and could see *what* a person gave.

Jesus' teaching portrays a huge contrast between the widow and the wealthy. The wealthy give large sums, but they can afford to do so (21:4). Jesus' criticism of the show-off wealthy teachers of the law is not that they are wealthy, but that they have become wealthy at the expense of widows (20:46–47) – like this widow who gave (21:2). Widows lacked a husband who could provide for them and frequently fell into poverty or prostitution. Some biblical laws are designed to protect them (e.g. Deuteronomy 14:28–29), and the prophets criticise rulers who do not do so (e.g. Isaiah 1:23; 10:1–2). The wealthy teachers' behaviour flatly contradicts their professed piety, for they oppress the weak and needy, including widows – and will face God's judgement as a result (20:47).

The widow's giving 'all she had to live on' (21:4) has two implications. First, she demonstrates her godliness by her readiness to give well beyond her means. She models the wholehearted discipleship to which Jesus calls his followers, putting giving to God as the top priority for her money – it's not what she gives, in absolute terms, but the devotion which her generosity bespeaks, which is significant.

Second, the juxtaposition of 20:46–47 with the story of the widow (21:1–4) implies that her situation may be a result of the wealthy teachers' unscrupulous actions. She lives in poverty as a widow: the two small coins (21:2) are literally 'all that she has to live on'. This is an injustice which should not happen within Israel, for the hope was that no one would be in need, because of the generosity of God's people to each other (Deuteronomy 15:4–8). Strikingly, widows were a group the earliest Christians made a priority to care for (e.g. Acts 6:1–6), and thus 'there was not a needy person among them' (Acts 4:34). Economic oppression is inimical to the life of the people of God.

Guidelines

Luke 20 calls us to consider these remarkable, unrepeatable events in their uniqueness. They have, of course, implications for how we live as Christians today, but those implications flow from reading the stories in all their distinctiveness in first-century Jerusalem.

Jesus' authority presents a huge challenge to the Jewish leaders (vv. 1–8), especially as he confronts them about their holding on to their positions of delegated authority as teachers of the law. But they and their ancestors are the wicked tenants who want the master's vineyard for themselves, to the extent that they will kill the son (vv. 9–16, 19). When they seek to get him to condemn himself by the question about paying taxes to the emperor, Jesus turns the question round and makes it clear that God's demands come first (vv. 21–26). He knows the scriptures and teaches with authority about the world to come in response to the Sadducees (vv. 27–38). And when all are silent, Jesus asks his own question about the Messiah who is David's Lord as well as David's son (vv. 41–44). Because he is who he is, he speaks with authority about right behaviour going with right teaching, with a sharp dig at the teachers (vv. 45–47).

How can we think of Jesus? He presents himself as God's son, the Messiah, but not the kind of Messiah the people of his day expected. He is not only a descendant of David, but also greater than David as his 'Lord'. As Israel's true king, he represents Israel, but he is obedient to God in a way no Israelite king ever was or could be. From eternity, he has been Lord of all and now, living as a human being, he is all that Israel – and her king – were meant to be. He is fully and perfectly human, as well as being fully and perfectly Lord.

Luke portrays our proper response to this extraordinary Jesus both positively and negatively at the end of the section we have been reading. Negatively, it is not to be people who say one thing and live differently, teaching 'the truth' but living a lie by oppressing people in need (20:45–47). Positively, it is to give 'all we have to live on' into Jesus' hands, including our bodies, wills, minds and gifts (21:4). What are the areas of your handling of these things which you need to consider?

1 The failing and falling temple

Luke 21:5–11

The Jerusalem temple was a huge and impressive building, and was expanding to double its size during Jesus' lifetime. Herod the Great had begun the work in 20BC, and it would go on until AD62. Some stones used were massive, weighing up to 100 tons (they are still visible today). The expanded temple's total 'footprint' was over 35 football fields, and its walls reached 80 feet (24.4 metres) high. No wonder people thought it impressive (v. 5)!

Jesus' response must have been startling: the temple was so big and solid that it would be hard to envisage its reduction to rubble (v. 6; see 19:42–44). It was so provocative that people in the temple courts asked Jesus about it – the questioners are not disciples, for no disciple in Luke ever addresses Jesus as 'Teacher' (v. 7). Their question is about 'these things', that is, the events Jesus spoke about (v. 6), and the rest of this chapter comprises his answer.

Jesus' answer begins with a sketch of the conditions of the period leading up to the temple's destruction (vv. 8–11). We know of many such events in that period from the late first-century Jewish historian Josephus: people claiming to be prophets or messiahs or kings; wars and uprisings against the Romans; famines, epidemics and earthquakes; and signs in the skies (i.e. from heaven, v. 11) understood as the gods speaking.

A key sign of the coming destruction of the temple will be '*a* nation will rise against *a* nation, and *a* kingdom against *a* kingdom' (v. 10, my translation). It was not the general, although scary, features of tumult (vv. 8–9) which signalled 'the end' of the temple (v. 9); rather, a specific nation rising against another – when the Jewish nation revolted against Rome – was the key signal that the temple's end was near. That was to be so: the Jewish war against Rome began in AD66, and the city fell in AD70.

Jesus does not want his disciples to be taken by surprise, and so he announces events in advance. His purpose, as we shall see, is not to encourage speculation about the timing or significance of historical events, but to call his disciples to faithfulness in the midst of what God is doing in and through history.

2 Living in difficult times

Jesus turns from describing the characteristics of the period leading to the temple's destruction (21:8–11) to calling his disciples to respond rightly in these difficult times. This section has many echoes in Acts, where the believers face and meet the challenges Jesus outlines.

Before the run-up to the temple's end, the disciples will face persecution and will have to answer for their faith ('because of my name', v. 12). The list fits the picture in Acts, where the believers are put under pressure in Jewish contexts (Acts 4:17–18), thrown into prison (Acts 4:1–3) and speak before kings and (Roman) governors (Acts 18:12–17; 23:33—24:27; 25:1—26:32). Jesus warns them now that this will happen, so that they will not be taken by surprise but will recognise these opportunities to bear witness to him (v. 13) – and the story Acts tells is of them doing exactly that (see King Agrippa's recognition of this, Acts 26:28).

How will they not buckle under such pressure? What resources will enable them to stay faithful when even their families turn against them (v. 16)? Jesus' answer is that he will equip them with 'words and a wisdom' for the situation (vv. 14–15). This is remarkable, for it assumes that during the period in which Jesus is no longer physically present, he will continue to empower the disciples. He will not be absent but will still be actively involved in the proclamation of the message. Jesus has already said to the disciples that the Spirit will enable them to speak powerfully and effectively in such situations (12:11–12); the combination with this statement is very striking, for it means that Jesus is still active after his death – both by the Spirit and by acting himself from his place of authority at God's right side (e.g. Acts 7:55–56; 9:3–6, 34).

It would be possible to read verse 18 in isolation as Jesus giving a 'blank cheque' promise that the disciples will not suffer. The surrounding words are so clear that they *will* suffer (vv. 12, 16–17) that Jesus' promise cannot be a guarantee that they will not be physically or emotionally harmed; but their ultimate fate is secure if they will remain faithful to him (v. 19). Jesus doesn't promise a smooth journey, just a safe arrival.

3 Earth-shattering events and their meaning

Luke 21:20–28

Jesus resumes his answer to the question of when the temple will fall (21:7), and answers in terms of the events to come (vv. 20–24) and their significance (vv. 25–28).

In one sense, having Jerusalem surrounded by military might is hardly a surprising sign of the temple's fall (v. 20). Josephus gives a horrific account of the Roman siege, designed to starve the city into submission. It included famine so severe that people harmed and killed others to get food, even within a family – the most vulnerable suffered most (vv. 21, 23–24).

Although this was a truly dreadful prospect, its significance was worse, for Jesus calls it 'punishment' (v. 22; NRSV 'vengeance'), echoing Hosea 9:7 (NIV): 'The days of punishment are coming, the days of reckoning are at hand.' Hosea was warning Israel because of their rejection of God's word through him. Further, there will be 'wrath against this people' (v. 23) – behind the Romans stands God's settled hostility against his people's rebellion, seen in the leaders' rejection of Jesus (see also 13:34–35; 19:42–44).

Jesus moves into symbolic language to explain the significance of these events further. The language of verses 25–28 draws on scripture, such as Isaiah 13:10 and 34:4. In such passages, the prophet is not speaking of the end of the space-time universe, but uses pictorial language to show how significant the events were to be – they were signs of God's judgement on his people. When we describe an event as 'earth-shattering', we are saying that it is important and significant, not that the earth is being physically shattered.

So when Jesus turns to Daniel 7:13–14 to speak of the 'son of man', he follows Daniel's lead (v. 27; NRSV puts some words in quotation marks to show they come from Daniel 7). In Daniel 7, the son of man goes *from* earth to God, 'the Ancient of Days', and is given power and authority over all. The word translated 'coming' (v. 27) can also mean 'going', and the latter is the direction of travel in Daniel 7. So we should expect verse 27 to speak of the same reality – that Jesus will be recognised as the one who has been taken up to God's right side as ruler of all things. That is the sign to believers that they are secure and safe (v. 28).

4 Recognise the signs and believe the words!

Luke 21:29–33

By now, the crowds' heads must have been spinning and their minds boggling at what Jesus was saying: the temple was to be dismantled, the city was to fall and all this was judgement from God. How could they be ready for all of this, since the signs Jesus gives are either rather general (21:8–11) or so near in time to the fall of the city that it would be too late to do much else (21:20–24)?

Jesus tells a parable to explain: it's like the growth of a fig tree, which loses its leaves in the winter. When buds and then leaves appear on its branches in late spring, summer is near (vv. 29–30). The point of the parable is not to encourage speculation, but to call his hearers to open their eyes to what is going on. Jesus has given them sufficient indication of the run-up to Jerusalem's fall, and now they need to take notice of it.

God's rule (kingdom) will be seen in these cataclysmic events (v. 31), which will happen within the lifetime of those present (v. 32). In both sentences, Jesus speaks of 'these things', referring to the events of the fall of the city and the temple, and thus links to 'these things' in verse 28, which include the son of man's 'coming' to God to receive authority and power (21:27). Earlier, Jesus connected the coming of the son of man with God's rule becoming visible within his hearers' lifetime (9:26–27). The echo of the son of man from Daniel 7:13–14 in Luke 9 and 21 is likely, therefore, to refer to Jesus' resurrection and ascension, by which he is established as ruler of all. The 'times of the Gentiles' (21:24) will follow, when the believing community expands to embrace people from the whole earth, as the book of Acts narrates.

Jesus underlines the claims he is making by an even more remarkable claim: what he says is more solid, more dependable, than the ground on which his hearers stand (v. 33). His words are indestructible and thus utterly reliable – just like those of God (see Isaiah 40:8). In the end, it all depends on who you see Jesus as being.

5 Getting a right perspective on life

At this point in what Jesus says, there may be a shift from the fall of the temple into a period further in the future, for Jesus now speaks of 'that day' (v. 34), by contrast with 'these things' (21:28, 31–32). Further, 'that day' will affect everyone on earth (v. 35) and will be the time when Jesus' hearers will 'stand before the son of man' (v. 36). We may, in other words, now be hearing about the end of all things when Jesus returns, rather than only the period leading to Jerusalem's fall (see Acts 1:11 and compare Luke 12:39–40; 17:26–35). If so, Jesus' warnings are to do with the whole period between his ascension and his return.

Luke repeatedly warns of a limited perspective fixated on this life and this world, rather than a heavenly perspective. This danger stands behind Jesus' teaching about not hoarding wealth (12:15–21), and thus his call to be generous to people in need (12:32–34) – both exhort people to put God first, above wealth and possessions. Jesus here warns against this way of thinking and living as people wait for the events to come.

The word translated 'dissipation' or 'carousing' (v. 34) may well refer to a drunken hangover. Jesus portrays a culture where people are entertaining themselves to death, drinking themselves into a stupor and waking up with throbbing heads next morning. The loss of control in drunkenness prevents people being alert and ready, for alcohol is a depressant which dulls the senses.

It is not only excessive alcohol which is dangerous; 'the worries of this life' can have the same effect (v. 34). To be constantly attentive to what you need is to 'weigh down your heart' – just like drunkenness. At the time of Moses, Pharaoh had a weighed-down (often translated 'hardened') heart, and it caused him to oppose God's plans (Exodus 7:14; 8:15, 19, 32; 9:7, 34–35), and to be taken by surprise when God delivered Israel.

Jesus calls his audience not to have such a heart, but instead to watch by praying (v. 36). To pray is to open our lives to God's voice, intervention and direction. A perspective distorted by alcohol or our daily needs is put right as we pray, for through prayer we place our lives into God's hands.

6 Summing up and looking forward

We will shortly enter the climax of Luke's gospel, the last hours of Jesus' life when he will hang between heaven and earth on the cross to save Israel and all humanity. Luke brings this part of his book to a close with three snapshots of what we have been seeing since Jesus arrived in Jerusalem.

First, we see Jesus at his regular activities: day by day, he teaches in the temple; evening by evening, he walks out of the city to the Mount of Olives to rest (21:37). It is likely that he is staying with his friends Mary, Martha and Lazarus in Bethany, located near the Mount, about two miles (3 kilometres) east of Jerusalem (10:38–42; John 11:1). The Mount of Olives is also the site of Gethsemane, where Jesus goes to pray on his last night (22:39–42 – the name of the site is given by Mark 14:32), which suggests how Judas knew where to take the arrest party (22:47). Jesus has spoken to his disciples of what is coming (18:31–33) and, knowing this, he does not change his behaviour: God has called him to teach, and God has called him – like all people – to rest; so he does these things.

Second, the reaction of the people to Jesus is that they get up early to hear Jesus teach (21:38). His hours of teaching were probably from early until late morning, when the day became too hot for people to stay in the temple courts. 'The people' include the massive number of Passover pilgrims who came for the festival (22:1) – the city's population swelled by six- or seven-fold. These faithful Jews drank in Jesus' teaching.

Third, by contrast with the Passover pilgrims, the Jewish leaders continue to plot against Jesus (22:2; see 19:47; 20:1, 19). The chief priests would find Jesus' teaching about the temple's destruction (21:6) particularly unacceptable, and the teachers of the law would remember Jesus' criticisms of them (20:45–47). The problem they face is the crowds, who welcome Jesus and love his teaching (19:48; 20:6, 19; 21:38). What to do?

And all of this is going on at Passover (22:1), the time when the Jews remembered God saving them from slavery in Egypt in Moses' day through the death of the Passover lambs (Exodus 12:3, 7, 12–13). The festival itself points forwards to what Jesus will accomplish through his death.

Guidelines

Our temptation when listening to Jesus' predictions about the future is to get into constructing timelines of events and making forecasts, whatever view we take of the meaning of Jesus' words here. Jesus' predictions and warnings in Luke 21 are much debated, and in these notes I have taken one view of their interpretation. Space is too limited to offer a full justification for this reading: you can read more on this, and other views, in the commentaries.

The key to reading this passage, however, is not to speculate about the future and try to nail down what particular things are and when they might happen. Jesus' intention is clear: he is teaching to help his followers know how to live during the period he speaks about. It seems those present took his advice, for the church historian Eusebius reports that believers in Jerusalem fled to Pella in Transjordan when they knew the Romans were approaching (vv. 20–21).

The believers were to face great suffering for their commitment to follow Jesus (vv. 12, 16–17), as has been the case throughout the church's history. Today, more Christians suffer for their faith than ever before, and even in western countries apathy or open hostility towards the exclusive claims of the Christian faith is widespread. Jesus' promise of words and wisdom to persecuted and suffering believers (vv. 14–15) is highly relevant to these believers, and gives us ways to pray for them. Why not learn about some of the ways believers suffer for their faith today and make it your aim – perhaps with others – to pray regularly for them? A number of Christian organisations provide valuable information and prayer fuel in print and on their websites, such as:

- Christian Solidarity Worldwide: **csw.org.uk**
- Open Doors: **opendoorsuk.org**
- Release International: **releaseinternational.org**

Dear Lord, please protect our brothers and sisters around the world who are being persecuted for their faith, especially those who are active in sharing the gospel. Let your peace reign on those regions where your children are not permitted the freedom to live out their faith in safety. Watch over and encourage those who work to support oppressed believers on the ground, risking their own lives to do so. In Jesus' name. Amen

FURTHER READING

James R. Edwards, *The Gospel according to Luke (Pillar NT Commentary)* (Eerdmans, 2015) – a meatier commentary for those who want to dig deeper.

R.T. France, *Luke (Teach the Text)* (Baker, 2013) – a wonderful commentary with good explanations of the text and helpful ideas for preaching and teaching.

Tom Wright, *Luke for Everyone* (SPCK, 2001) – clear, thoughtful devotional reading of the whole gospel.

Like a tree, planted…

Neil Le Tissier

It seems to me that nothing livens up the written word, and helps broaden insight and understanding, quite like a well-chosen metaphor. But what is metaphor? And does it have any rightful place in communicating the nature of God, faith and biblical truth? After all, what's wrong with good old-fashioned plain speaking (and writing)? Or is there a danger that without it we 'be ever hearing, but never understanding; be ever seeing, but never perceiving' (Isaiah 6:9)?

Over time, metaphor has come to be understood as more than a descriptive tool whereby an *image* is substituted for a *fact* about a subject in order that the subject be understood more clearly. Interaction theorists have suggested that new ways of understanding open up when the *image* and *fact* collide unexpectedly, causing the reader to look afresh at the passage and allowing the text to impact at a newer, deeper level. The text is then carrying out more than an *informative* function; it also takes on a *performative* one that causes the reader to feel tension, to analyse why and to choose how to respond.

It shouldn't surprise us, therefore, that the Bible is packed with metaphors; they are an important means of engaging and involving the reader. A popular one is the tree, because this important biblical symbol crosses temporal and cultural boundaries with ease. The tree is seen as majestic, strong, fruit-bearing, health-giving and shade-providing, a perfect image of hope and security. But it is also associated with idolatry, arrogance, famine, judgement and fire. The arboreal metaphor has a tension at its core, causing the reader to examine again where their dependence lies.

This week, we will examine a selection of its scriptural uses, and the challenges they pose.

Unless otherwise stated, Bible quotations are from the New International Version (1984).

1 Paradise

Genesis 2:4–17

The Lord planted a garden in Eden (v. 8). Our word 'paradise' comes from an ancient Persian term *pairi-daëza*, which meant 'enclosure', and later 'park' or 'garden'. These pleasure gardens were walled-in or hedged-around, and full of trees. The name gave rise to the Greek term *paradeisos*, which is used in Revelation 2:7 to refer to 'the paradise of God', where the one who overcomes can 'eat from the tree of life'.

Eden was full of 'all kinds of trees… that were pleasing to the eye and good for food' (v. 9). It was a well-watered, very fruitful and shady idyll where the Lord himself walked, enjoying his creation. What a beautiful image of the blissful presence, abundant provision and original purpose of God. And central to it all was this same tree of life. In both gardens, it symbolises abundance, fruitfulness, security, peace and freedom. The fruit would nourish them, and the leaves bring healing (Revelation 22:2). God's desired relationship with his creation has no bounds nor indeed a time limit.

But with all this privilege comes responsibility. Adam and Eve were to work the garden and take care of it – not as a means of securing this privilege; rather, as a right and natural response to it. They were created to share in God's work. And this is not to be confused with the 'toil' that will come outside the garden; this is life in all its fullness.

Many people regard work as toil, and see it as blood, sweat and tears that must be shed in order to gain a little reward. However, the garden metaphor, with its abundant and fruitful trees, suggests not. Rather, the picture is of God's desire to work with us, to be creative together and then to walk and talk together in the cool of the day.

Of course, we live outside the garden and paradise was lost. But for those who overcome, it will be restored, and the tree of life will be accessible once more. In the meantime, God's desire to work with us and be creative together has not changed. He still longs to walk and talk with us, to enjoy those refreshing encounters with us in the cool of the day, but he also longs to work with us creatively in whatever tasks he has given us to do. Paradise and work can still be synonymous in God's economy, but for us they are so often in tension.

2 Disobedience

At the centre of God's woodland paradise were two named trees. Beside the tree of life was the tree of the knowledge of good and evil but, in contrast with all the other trees, its fruit was strictly forbidden. The consequence of eating it was certain death (v. 3). The presence of such forbidden fruit in God's perfect place has given rise to one of our faith's FAQs: why did God put it there?

Metaphorically, these two key trees stand side-by-side as a reminder that at the heart of our relationship with God is freedom and choice. On the one hand, he has promised to provide all that we need and seeks a relationship based on complete trust. On the other hand, he desires that we choose to enter that relationship of our own free will, and not because there is no alternative.

So at the heart of the garden (and indeed the metaphor) is a tension between trust and wisdom. Is desiring wisdom such a bad thing? Is there a distinction between wisdom and knowledge? Is it a bad thing to seek to be wise and knowledgeable? Some Bible commentators suggest that the expression 'good and evil' is a merism: a figure of speech in which two extremes are used to encompass a whole concept. Others add that the reference here is to much more than intellectual knowledge; rather, it is to divine knowledge, to that which only God can know and fully understand. To seek this is to seek to be as God, and to be familiar with the mysteries that lie beyond us (Isaiah 55:9).

Scripture's wisdom literature encourages us to 'trust in the Lord with all your heart and lean not on your own understanding; in all your ways acknowledge him, and he will make your paths straight' (Proverbs 3:5–6). God's desire for us is not that we live in ignorance and blind faith, but that we rely on his guidance, his power and his resources, rather than our own.

And therein lies a major tension for many of us, perhaps. How do we grow in wisdom, intellect and understanding, while remaining reliant upon God for guidance and revelation? How do we become capable, resourceful and resilient individuals, while trusting fully in God's provision and power? There's surely a fine line between them, and one which is a daily challenge to walk.

3 Restoration

Adam and Eve succumbed to the tempter and were banished from the garden, and access to the tree of life and its eternal benefit was denied them by the sword-wielding cherubim. Outside paradise, life would be marked by pain, toil, sweat and death (Genesis 3:16–19), but 'to him who overcomes, I will give the right to eat from the tree of life' (Revelation 2:7). So what is to be overcome, and how?

Paul writes to the church in Rome, 'Sin entered the world through one man, and death through sin' (v. 12), and, 'For the wages of sin is death, but the gift of God is eternal life in Christ Jesus our Lord' (6:23). Overcoming is not within our ability, but as we choose to put our trust in God, he makes it possible through the sacrificial gift of his Son on another tree, the cross.

Speaking of the cross as a tree may seem rather old-fashioned and quaint, a throwback to the poetic hymn-writing of a former generation. However, there is a strong scriptural basis to this image. In Deuteronomy 21:23, we read that 'anyone who is hung on a tree is under God's curse'. This image is taken up by Peter in Acts 5:30, 10:39 and 13:29 and 1 Peter 2:24, to refer to Jesus' crucifixion; and in Galatians 3:13, Paul specifically refers the reader back to the Deuteronomy passage to explain why Christ needed to become 'a curse for us'. Both could have chosen the more common Greek word for cross (*stauros*), but instead they used *xulon* ('tree'), which appears in the Septuagint version of Deuteronomy 21:23. Even John chose *xulon* over the more usual word *dendron* to refer to the tree of life in Revelation.

Surely it's not a coincidence that the tree metaphor should link Eden's trees, and the choice they represent, with the cursed cross and God's generous gift of a way back to himself. It wonderfully expresses the tension that exists between seeking to be the best we can be, while still trusting fully in God and following his ways. We all have a choice to make over who is Lord of our lives, and then to exercise that choice daily. For those of us who have given our lives to God, how often do we take back the reins? Thankfully, while the tree is a symbol of judgement, it is also a symbol of hope and of redeeming forgiveness.

4 Idolatry

Deuteronomy 12:1–32

As the Israelites stood on the threshold of the promised land, Moses warned them about the places where the pagan peoples worshipped their gods 'under every spreading tree' (v. 2). While this expression probably began with specific locations in mind, it became a euphemism for any site where the 'detestable practices' of the pagans were carried out (1 Kings 14:23–24).

In the ancient Near East, the tree was seen as a representation of the divine. Its height, strength, beauty and regenerative power made it a natural icon, and so it held an important place in worship. The Canaanites had been worshipping Asherah, a fertility goddess, and had established a number of sacred sites on high places under the shade of large, leafy trees. Her portrayal was as a living tree that had been stylised with her image.

Early Israelite worship had included the planting of trees as an expression of gratitude to their faithful God (Genesis 21:33), and worship became established at those sacred places. Certain trees, such as 'the great tree of Moreh' (Genesis 12:6), 'the Palm of Deborah' (Judges 4:5) and 'the oak in Ophrah' (Judges 6:11), became known as places where God spoke with his people. When the temple was established, many trees were planted in and around it as living reminders of God's invisible, mysterious blessing that was at work among them.

So perhaps we shouldn't be too surprised that the Israelites regularly slipped into the pagan practices against which Moses, and the later prophets, warned. The tree would always encapsulate for them the fine line (and tension) between worshipping the creator and worshipping the places and things through which he chose to reveal himself.

Our Christian history is littered with examples of sacred places and artefacts which take on a greater importance than God intended. Even today, we can think of many examples of where the things (places and practices) that God has chosen as his channel of communication, and his means of revelation, have become more precious to us than was ever intended. And I wouldn't doubt many of us have experienced churches where they are more passionate about the *way* they worship than about the *one* they worship. As the Israelites discovered, and we would do well to remember, idolatry can be a very subtle thing.

5 Consequences

Isaiah 1:21–31

Despite all that God had done for his people Israel, they were a constant source of disappointment, as they fell repeatedly into idolatry. So he sent one prophet after another to point out their foolishness, and the tree metaphor appears regularly to portray their pride and self-centredness – and its consequences.

Because of the 'sacred oaks in which you have delighted', Isaiah warns them that they will become 'like an oak with fading leaves' (vv. 29–30). Their obsession with themselves will cut them off from the life-giving water, and this will render them as tinder. As such, they will become susceptible to the fire which no one can quench.

In Isaiah 5:1–7, the prophet uses a metaphorical parable about a friend's vineyard to convey the owner's bewilderment when his 'choicest vines' produce nothing but 'bad fruit' (v. 2). The parable's hearers are naturally not surprised when he pulls down its protective hedge and allows it to become a wasteland – until, that is, they realise they are that vineyard and the owner is God. Jeremiah also uses the vine metaphor to express the incredulity that 'a choice vine of sound and reliable stock' could become 'a corrupt, wild vine' (Jeremiah 2:21). And Jesus uses this metaphor most dramatically in his warning in John 15.

In Isaiah 2:12–13, the prophet addresses 'all the proud and lofty' as 'the cedars of Lebanon' and makes it clear that they will be 'felled' and 'brought low' (10:33). As Proverbs puts it, 'Pride goes before destruction, a haughty spirit before a fall' (16:18).

The prophets are not so much emphasising God's punishment, as though he is lashing out in petulant anger, but they are expressing the consequences of the poor choices the people have made and their self-destructive behaviour.

There are times, perhaps, when we find ourselves on something of a pedestal. Often, in church circles, it's because others have placed us there, rather than by our own choice. But if we're honest, isn't there a feel-good factor when we're up there? And perhaps there are times when we are overly concerned with our personal needs, rights, desires and opinions; and the decisions we then make become poor because we've not been concerned enough to consider God's choices and other people's needs.

The tree is a mighty and beautiful thing, but susceptible nonetheless to the axe and fire.

6 Hope

Isaiah 11:1–11

The tree is a wonderful image of hope, with its innate ability to sprout new life from a seemingly dead stump. Neither axe nor fire can rob a tree of its life as long as the roots are intact and there is a source of water. Indeed, the new growth is arguably stronger and more fruitful than the old.

Job takes up this theme, emphasising the need for even 'the scent of water' for it to produce buds, such is the revitalising combination of rootedness and access to water (Job 14:7–10). Sadly, his words in Job 19:10 express his sense of uprooted hopelessness, but the story ends with a confirmation that in holding on to God, all will be well in the end.

In Hosea 14:4–7, the prophet speaks words of hope over Israel. God will be like the dew to them if they will send down their roots. Young shoots will grow and they will be as the splendour of the olive tree and the fragrance of the cedar. They will blossom like the vine.

Jesus uses the vine metaphor to emphasise the need for us as branches to remain in him so that we might bear much fruit (John 15:1–17), otherwise we will be cut off and thrown into the fire. Even fruitful branches will be pruned, in order that we might produce more and better fruit. This tension between being *cut back* and being *cut off* expresses most emphatically the challenge at the heart of the metaphor. We have a choice: to put our trust in God, to seek his ways and to follow in obedience; or to put our trust in ourselves, to rely on our own understanding and to build with our own abilities.

The psalmist sums up God's desire for us. God blesses the one who delights in his ways and seeks to follow them daily: 'He is like a tree planted by streams of water, which yields its fruit in season and whose leaf does not wither. Whatever he does prospers' (Psalm 1:3).

Guidelines

One of my favourite passages in scripture is found in Jeremiah 17:7–8 (NIV, 2011): 'Blessed is the one who trusts in the Lord, whose confidence is in him. They will be like a tree planted by the water that sends out its roots by the stream. It does not fear when heat comes; its leaves are always green. It has no worries in a year of drought and never fails to bear fruit.'

What a wonderful image! Don't we long to be like that tree, displaying such faith, rootedness, security and fruitfulness?

And yet, across scripture, doesn't this metaphor also challenge us and make us feel uncomfortable? For there is surely a fine line between standing firm and growing strong in the Lord, and being lofty and proud. And even when we spot that subtle difference, aren't we still susceptible to being 'placed on a pedestal' by others, especially when exercising a more obvious ministry? Isn't there also a risk that we give too much focus and emphasis on *how* we worship, than on *who* we worship? And are we sometimes so caught up in a hunger to know more and understand better that we find ourselves seeking after wisdom more than faith?

Thankfully, the tree reminds us too of Christ's sacrifice, the hope of a restored relationship and renewed call. Its ability to put out new shoots from even the most damaged or heavily-pruned stump has been a source of great relief to me – a ham-fisted gardener!

There is a tension at the heart of this metaphor, but one which I believe keeps us aware of both the pitfalls and the privileges of service. My prayer is that we walk that tightrope carefully.

FURTHER READING

Walter Brueggemann, '"Vine and Fig Tree": A case study in imagination and criticism', *Catholic Biblical Quarterly 43* (1981), pp. 188–204.

George Caird, *The Language and Imagery of the Bible* (Gerald Duckworth & Co Ltd, 1980).

Colin Gunton, *The Actuality of Atonement: A study of metaphor, rationality and the Christian tradition* (T & T Clark, 1988).

Kirsten Nielsen, *There is Hope for a Tree: The tree as metaphor in Isaiah* (JSOT Press, 1989).

1 Chronicles

Henry Wansbrough OSB

The first question to be asked about 1 Chronicles is why the unknown author wrote this account. In the Hebrew Bible it is called 'The Events of Days', suggesting a sort of world history. The descriptive name Chronicle was given by Jerome, who translated it into Latin in the early fifth century AD. It is divided into two books simply for convenience, since the piece is too long to fit on a single scroll. The historical period covered is that of the Israelite monarchy, but interest is centred on the temple rather than the kings who reigned during that time. The detailed descriptions of temple liturgy and functionaries leave no doubt that the principal purpose is to glorify the importance of the temple liturgy in Judaism, restored after the Babylonian exile, and to express the author's delight in that liturgy.

The basic facts of the history are, in all but a very few instances, taken from the earlier historical books Samuel and Kings. However, the narrative has been sapped of most of the interesting human motivations and character which make for such gripping reading. The moral lessons presented in those books have also disappeared, for the earlier account was carefully shaped to teach a fourfold cycle: the infidelity of Israel, leading to punishment, and then repentance by the Israelites, leading to liberation by a forgiving God. That lesson is given in its fullest form by the book of Deuteronomy, which earned the name 'the Deuteronomic history' for the historical account. Most national histories are a record of success, but the Deuteronomic history is a record of human failure and divine forgiveness. These are replaced in 1 Chronicles by a fascination with the temple liturgy in all its detail. Nevertheless, in considering the history of the gradual process which lies behind the establishment of the liturgy, we must consider how God is to be seen in the events and people which lead to it.

When was it written? All we can say for sure is that it must have been written after the rebuilding of the temple and the re-establishment of the temple liturgy after the return of the exiles from Babylon in the late sixth century BC.

Unless otherwise stated, scripture quotations are from the Revised New Jerusalem Bible, which has been translated by me.

1 The peopling of the world

1 Chronicles 1:1–16

The beginning of this story may seem a meaningless jangle of strange names, but to someone impregnated with the Jewish tradition it is a thrilling drum roll. The very mention of the names of the ancestors at the beginning of biblical history would have stirred a chord. There is a similar drum roll in the genealogy at the beginning of the gospel of Matthew, leading from Abraham to Joseph, the adoptive father of Jesus, invoking the memory of the great figures of Israelite history. The verses with which Chronicles begins function in a different key, a geographical rather than a historical spread, using the data of Genesis 5 and 10 to claim the whole known world for Israel. These are not intended to give father–son relationships in the modern sense of the word, but racial groupings as a matter of descent.

The first four verses of our reading are a reminder of the decline of humanity after Adam, for a feature of the personalities of Genesis 5 is the sharp decline in the length of life of these patriarchs. The blessing of long life declines from Adam's 930 years, to Seth's 912, Enosh's 905, a hump for Methuselah to 969, then only 777 for Lamech.

The geographical spread begins with the sons of Noah. First come really distant nations, including Medes and Greeks (represented by Javan, or Ionia, and Kittim) and the mythically distant Tarshish (sometimes thought to be Tartessos in Spain). Then, from the sons of Ham, we have the more familiar Cush (Ethiopia), Misraim (Egypt) and Canaan itself, the country into which the Hebrews moved from their slavery in Egypt. All these are lands with which Israel had familiar dealings. Misraim/Egypt's sons ominously include Caphtor, from which the bitter Philistine enemies of Israel will come. Familiar among Canaan's sons are the great coastal city of Sidon to the north and Jerusalem, the Jebusite city which was to be conquered by David and become the site of the temple.

For a record from a time when maps were unknown and travel restricted, this is a stirring list. These places were not, of course, subject to or dominated by Israel. But the list stemming from Adam claims for Israel the patronage of all these lands. For the little group of returned exiles, huddled round Jerusalem, this was an inspiring and reassuring claim. The rest of this chapter and the next will establish the links of the chain connecting to David, the principal hero of 1 Chronicles.

2 The sons of David

1 Chronicles 3:1–9

More than any other passage in 1 Chronicles, this short passage on David's children throbs with the complex story of David's rise to power and, yes, his fall. The books of Samuel give us the story from David's point of view, almost a propaganda version, beneath which one can discern an ambitious young warrior, making a name and power base for himself at the expense of Saul's family. By the time he was crowned king of the southern part of the country at Hebron, he had acquired two powerful wives: Abigail, the widow of a rich landowner of Judah, and Ahinoam. The only other time the name Ahinoam occurs in the Bible, it designates the wife of Saul; did David secure his power base by poaching his master's wife? Kings were not yet expected to be monogamous. The remainder of the list shows that dynastic marriage was an extra source of power.

However, it is the last name on the list, Tamar, which introduces tragedy and dissension. She was raped by her half-brother Amnon. When David took no action, her full brother Absalom revenged her by killing Amnon. Again, David was indecisive or indulgent, and allowed Absalom back into court after an all-too-brief period of exile. So, in his turn, Absalom built up his own power base and rebelled against his father, driving him out of Jerusalem. Even when his strengthened force confronted the rebels, David begged his army to keep his rebel son from harm. Again, in extreme old age, David's yielding to the blandishments of his favourite wife turned the succession to his throne into a bloodbath.

Why, then, was he revered as the great king? Was it as the founder of the temple liturgy because he seized the land on which the temple would be built – though, as a 'man of blood', he was forbidden to build it himself (1 Chronicles 28:3)? Was it as the founder of a dynasty and a line of kings to which were made the promises of an eternal kingship which would usher in the eschatological reign of peace (2 Samuel 7:5–16)? Or was it as the icon of repentance, responding with wholehearted contrition to Nathan's rebuke for adultery with Bathsheba and the callous murder of her husband, Uriah

(2 Samuel 12:13)? If the history of Israel is a story of sin and repentance, David, the passionate lover, sums it up and stands at its head.

3 The noble line of kings

1 Chronicles 3:10–24

It is hard to read this genealogical record of the royal house of David and Solomon without shedding a tear: it starts so well and ends so badly. For the author, the overriding importance is to establish the continuity between David and the present regime of the temple. The list starts with Solomon, that almost fabulous emperor. His empire covered most of the ancient Near East. His wisdom was enshrined in collections of countless proverbs. His wealth, which dazzled even the Queen of Sheba, was acquired by precious metals and as middleman for the sale of horses from Asia Minor to Egypt and chariots from Egypt to Asia Minor. But, too soon, we descend into the welter of puppet-monarchs before the exile, whose futile struggles to resist had no hope of withstanding the repeated onslaughts of the Babylonian war machine.

Perhaps most tragic of all is 'Jeconiah, the captive' (v. 17). The last thing he saw before his eyes were put out was the slaughter of his sons at the order of the King of Babylon. Then he was held captive in Babylon under house arrest for 37 years (2 Kings 25:27). Tragically, a schedule for the delivery of oil to this royal captive has been found on a Babylonian clay tablet. After Jeconiah, there follows a list of nobodies, whose only interest is to establish continuity to the official of the temple restored after King Cyrus set all the captives free to return and worship their own gods – and his successors provided the timbers and paid for the rebuilding.

Offsetting this miserable history is a touching recurrent feature in the names: the frequency with which the names end in 'iah'. This is a shorter version of the divine name whose consonants are YHWH. We do not know how this name was pronounced, for in Hebrew only the consonants are written; while Hebrew was still a living, spoken language, the vowels were simply known to everyone. No prizes for guessing what cities are meant by LNDN, CRDFF or GLSGW! The divine name in full was too majestic and awesome to be pronounced, and also too intimate to be bandied around in public – like the affectionate pet name which every parent and child has within the family. To avoid speaking the name, it was usual to say 'the Lord'.

This shortened name was combined with another word, so that 'Zedekiah' (v. 15) means 'the justice of the Lord' and 'Rephaiah' (v. 21) means 'the healing of the Lord'.

4 The death of Saul

1 Chronicles 10:1–14

With this tragic story of the death of Saul, a new method and a new approach begins. Up to now, the concentration has been on genealogies, in a determination to show the continuity between the new Israel and the old, particularly in the matter of temple personnel. All the officials and ministers in the restored temple earn their right to serve through their ancestry. Now, for the first time, we have an actual story! It is taken almost word for word from the final chapter of 1 Samuel, but the small differences are significant.

The terrible pathos of the account in 1 Samuel came from Saul's bewildered despair. He had been rejected by the Lord. Not knowing where to turn, he had consulted the Witch of En-Dor, despite his own recent prohibition of consulting such mediums. She had conjured up for him the spirit of Samuel, who had – to Saul's utter consternation – confirmed Saul's coming fate. Then, in two slightly different versions, came the inevitable disaster on the slopes of Mount Gilboa. Gilboa is still a tragic and eerie place, infested with trigger-happy Israeli border guards: a fitting scene for Saul's courageous death.

The author of Chronicles stresses the annihilation of Saul 'and all his House altogether' (v. 6; despite the contradiction of the previous lists of his descendants in 8:33–40) as a springboard for the newness of David. Saul's final humiliation is underlined by his head being fastened up in the temple of Dagon, the Philistine god, making it less likely that his brave and devoted supporters from Gilead would manage to grab his head and bury it with the rest of his body at Jabesh. The Philistine country (around the modern Tel Aviv) is several days' march from Jabesh, instead of the dozen kilometres from Jabesh to Beth Shean. The rejection of Saul is completed by explanation of the reason for it: failure to keep the word of the Lord and to consult the Lord. Saul's failure is definitively and brutally emphasised by the divine judgement, that God 'killed him' (v. 14).

This dark picture is all designed to contrast with the burst of light depicted in the rise of David. But it is significant that there is no mention of the swift execution of the messenger who brought David the news that he had killed the Lord's anointed (2 Samuel 1:13–16). The emphasis is on the temple rather than the monarchy.

5 David's leadership

1 Chronicles 11:15–19

The contrast between the way the story of David is told here and in the historical books of Samuel is striking. In Samuel, we find a long and arduous (not to say crooked) struggle to gain power, David laboriously building up his power base in the south of the country before being crowned king of the south at Hebron, and then seven years before the conquest of and coronation at Jerusalem. In Chronicles, it all happens in a rush, capped by lists of eager supporters. The whole country is clamouring to declare their loyalty to David.

The little story in today's reading stands out as an example of David's charismatic leadership. About this power of leadership there is no doubt. Jonathan falls under his spell to the extent of passing over to him his own Crown Prince's uniform, and further risks his father's anger. Michal, Saul's daughter, begs to marry him, and even deceives her father by putting a dummy in David's bed to divert his pursuers. The women of Israel dance to the song, 'David has killed his tens of thousands' (1 Samuel 18:7). Saul's attempt to pin David to the wall with his spear was surely provoked by jealousy at David's popularity.

Commentators have criticised David's action in the little story here recounted, by saying that he should never have put his soldiers up to such a life-threatening risk. Perhaps there is room for another point of view: David let slip a longing for the water of his home-well at Bethlehem, the well with which he had grown up. With modern homogenised chemical water-systems, most of us have forgotten the variety of tastes of natural water. Three of his champions took it as a 'dare', broke their way through the Philistine lines – there and back – and presented the water to David. What should he do at such an act of courage and devotion? Scold them? Congratulate them on their daring? I find in the solution the brilliance of an inspired and inspiring leader: he denied them their satisfaction and shared their disappointment by denying himself the satisfaction of drinking. Instead, he offers the spoils to God, the author of all safety and success, while at the same time forbidding them ever to repeat such foolhardy daring. It is the same David who shrugged off Saul's heavy armour against Goliath, who spared Saul in the cave, who dribbled down his beard to convince the Philistine leaders that he was a harmless fool and who danced with such abandon before the ark of the Lord.

6 The return of the ark (1)

1 Chronicles 13:1–14

David's military and political rise to power advances in three wholly distinct stages. First, he is established as king in Hebron, ruling over Judah, the southern part of the inhabitable region of the country (not including the southern desert of the Negeb). Next he is accepted as king by the northern tribes, who had at first continued to support Saul's son, Mephibaal. The third stage is then crucial, and is David's own move: the capture of Jerusalem. The unconquered Jebusite city of Jerusalem, on the spine of the ridge running from north to south, controlled the passage between Israel and Judah. When David, with his private army (as 2 Samuel shows, though 1 Chronicles 11:4 attributes this to an army drawn from 'all Israel'), captures Jerusalem, he makes his own city the hinge between these two very different territories. But his real stroke of genius is to make his city God's city by bringing to it the ark of the covenant, the religious seal of the military success.

Since the covenant made with Moses, the ark had been the symbol of God's presence. On the desert journey, it had been housed in the tent of meeting outside the camp, being too holy to be kept within the camp. Moses would go out, watched by every man of Israel from their tent openings, to meet God there, to hear and receive God's word. There alone would he remove the veil which covered his face, touched, made calloused, by the glory of God. At first, in Israel, the ark resided in the sanctuary of Shiloh; there, God first spoke to the boy Samuel. When battle against the Philistines was desperate, the ark was taken out to battle to guarantee victory – only to be disastrously captured. When Eli heard the news, he fell back and died. To the wife of Phinehas, the news was worse than the death of her husband, and she named their child Ichabod, or 'Where is the glory?'

But the ark was an uncomfortable prize to the Philistines and, in city after city, it produced a plague of piles and mice. Eventually, they were driven to station it in the border-town of Kiriath-Jearim. David's master stroke was to retrieve it and bring it to his own city to make Jerusalem not only David's city but God's own city, the centre of worship. The holiness of the ark is again seen when the bearers let it tilt and Uzzah put out his hand to steady it. You don't offer God a hand, and Uzzah paid with his life for his temerity.

Guidelines

We have advanced by leaps and bounds from Adam to David, preparing for the foundation of the temple and its liturgy. It has hardly been continuous reading, for we have passed over long lists of names and territories. Boring to read, they are nevertheless important in establishing the overall divine control of the places and peoples of the world then known to Israel. They constitute a statement that the God of Israel has planned and laid out the peoples of the world to the advantage of his own people. The focus is now beginning to narrow and intensify as the author prepares for the foundation of the temple liturgy as the crowning summit of creation and the continuing response of a grateful people. For the Chronicler, this alone made sense of the universe and all that was in it. For the Christian, a higher Eucharist has taken its place.

1 The return of the ark (2)

1 Chronicles 15:25—16:3

The story of the return of the ark presents the Chronicler at his most ample. The move is transformed from a fairly simple event into a magnificent spectacle involving the whole people. In the original story, the first part of the move – from Baalah to the house of Obed-Edom – involved an escort of David's picked troops (the figure of 30,000 troops is an absurd but typical exaggeration), whereas in Chronicles 'the whole assembly of Israel', from the Shihor of Egypt to the Pass of Hamath, transforms it into a national liturgical procession. The holiness and awe of the occasion is stressed by the fact that all the participants must first sanctify themselves before approaching the ark. The original second part of the procession also seemed a fairly simple affair, but now there are lists of liturgical officials, and it is made quite clear that only Levites and above can get anywhere near the ark. Instead of David dancing for the Lord with wild abandon and incurring Michal's prudish rebuke, now he is wearing a cloak of fine linen and behaving with more dignity; Michal merely 'despises him in her heart' (v. 29). The departure of the crowds is delayed until the inauguration of the full liturgy, with morning and evening sacrifices, psalms and full temple orchestra (16:43, echoing the simpler 2 Samuel 6:19).

The importance of the event is, of course, immense. Even after the loss of the ark at the sack of Jerusalem by the Babylonians, the fact that the ark was once lodged in the temple provides the link between the second and the first temples. Once sanctified by the presence of the ark, the place is holy forever.

The magnificent procession of the whole people in all its splendour is a fitting celebration of the Lord of all the world. It is the first climax of the book, for which the author uses all his splendid resources to celebrate the arrival of the presence of God in the holy place which will be forever the divine residence and the guarantee of his favour. The two psalms which are combined to conclude the ceremony fittingly acclaim first the divine care of Israel during its earlier wanderings (Psalm 105), and second the debt of gratitude and honour owed to the Lord by heaven and earth and all they contain (Psalm 96).

There is more to come, for as yet the ark is lodged only in a tent, as it was throughout the desert wanderings. Even more magnificence will attend the building and dedication of the temple.

2 A line of kings

1 Chronicles 17:1–15

For Christians, this exchange between David and Nathan is one of the most central in the Hebrew Bible. It hides beneath the gentle pun on the two senses of 'house': the temple and the dynasty. It begins with David's rather touching discomfort that he is better housed than the ark of the Lord. But God is not going to be patronised by David building a house for him; rather, God will outdo David's offer by promising a far more permanent house. This promise becomes the basis not only of Christian hope but also of the hope of Israel, quoted again and again in the prayers of Israel, for example Psalm 89, and then in the New Testament canticles of Mary, Zechariah and (by implication) Simeon in the temple. The line of kings will issue in the kingship of God inaugurated by Christ the King.

There are three small but significant differences between the accounts of 2 Samuel and 1 Chronicles. First, in Samuel God has already granted David 'rest from all his enemies'; in Chronicles this would be inappropriate, because the following chapter will give an account of David's wars of conquest. Second, in Samuel God's reply to David's offer is more general, implying that no human being may build God a house, whereas in Chronicles it is simply that David is not the man to do it: David is a man of blood (was it the wars which disqualified him, or his murders of possible rivals in Saul's clan and of Bathsheba's husband?) and Solomon will be the builder of the temple. Third, the promise in Samuel foresees merely corrective, not destructive, punishment for future offences, whereas in Chronicles there is no suggestion of any need for punishment, merely the guarantee that this line will never, by contrast to Saul's line, be rejected. Dazzled by the splendour of the new temple, the author conveniently forgets the horrors of Israel's infidelity and punishment by exile.

In the books of Samuel, there are two touching occasions when David replies to God's action with a prayer. The first is here, when David responds by going in to the Lord and confessing his own nothingness as God's servant: 'Who am I, Lord God, that you have led me as far as this?' (2 Samuel

7:18). The second is at the death of the son born to Bathsheba. The son fell ill, and David tried by every means in his power to beg that he should live. But when the son dies, David simply goes into the temple and prostrates himself in a silent prayer of acceptance (2 Samuel 12:20–23). To these, the Chronicler adds David's great prayer in 1 Chronicles 29.

3 The insult to David's envoys

1 Chronicles 19:1–5

This little incident sets in motion David's policy of expansion outside the territory of Israel. We cannot now reconstruct what David's original motives were in sending these envoys. Was it no more than a friendly gesture of sympathy on a family bereavement? Was it a suggestion of superiority, inviting some response of submission? Was it the reconnaissance in preparation for attack, as Hanun's advisors suggested? In any case, the Ammonites were having none of it, and replied with a neat and calculated insult, an insult primarily not to the unfortunate envoys but to their principal, David himself. In those days, shaving was difficult and beards were normal, so the shaved face was probably intended to suggest that the envoys were kids too young to grow a beard, unless it was a wider reflection on their sexuality. In that male-dominated world, it could well have been a suggestion that all David's warriors were girls, incapable of fighting – a suggestion all too obviously belied by the drastic abbreviation of their tunics. In 2 Samuel 10:4, only half their beards were shaved, which would merely have made them look silly. In any case, they would have been a laughing stock to all who saw them. They would have been grateful for David's sympathetic reaction!

The wars sparked by this insult made David master of much of the territory of what is now the kingdom of Jordan. As is the custom with all victory claims, the Ammonite casualty figures are far too high for any reasonable estimate of population numbers at this time. Furthermore, the lack of any archaeological evidence (apart from a single inscription discovered in the 1990s) has suggested to some scholars that the whole idea of a Davidic empire is wishful thinking. Of greater interest to the Chronicler is that the blood shed in these operations contributed to the prohibition on David of building the temple, for he was a 'man of blood'. The Benjaminite Shimei gave him this sobriquet in 2 Samuel 16:7–8 for his heartless elimination of all able-bodied members of Saul's clan, leaving only Jonathan's crippled son. The evidence given in 2 Samuel 21:2–10 is insufficient to prove whether this was justified by the standards of the time, but the manner of its doing was certainly cold-bloodedly brutal. David was taking no risks of a rival claimant to the throne.

4 The threshing floor of Ornan

1 Chronicles 21:18–27

We have now arrived at the immediate preliminary to the building of the temple, the purchase of the land. But this extract needs an introduction.

David decides to hold a census of his people. In Chronicles, it is Satan who incites him to do this, whereas in 2 Samuel 24:1 the responsibility is put directly on God, although David is later criticised and blamed for taking the census. It is not at all clear why taking a census should be regarded as a crime deserving of such horrific punishment as the three alternatives between which David has to choose. The least unsatisfactory suggestion is that taking a census implies ownership of the people counted, whereas Israel are God's people and David has no right to assume ownership. However, the most important factor is that David is again the figure of the repentant sinner, as in the case of his adultery with Bathsheba and murder of her husband (narrated in 2 Samuel, but too shameful to be included in Chronicles). In both cases, David yields to temptation, but at the prompting of the prophet, repents and makes reparation. In this case, the prophet is Gad, and the reparation sets in motion the whole weighty process of building the temple – a process which makes it possible to regard David as the initiator of the temple.

An attractive feature elaborated by the Chronicler is the comparison to Abraham's purchase of a burial plot at Hebron for his dead wife, the first acquisition of territory in the Holy Land, the first fulfilment of the promise to Abraham. Such a modelling is a typical biblical way of showing the significance of an event: the similarity of detail shows a similarity of significance. In both cases, a member of the chosen people is acquiring land from a Gentile. In both cases, the Gentile offers to give the land freely (with some extras thrown in), but the member of the chosen people insists on paying a fair price – or rather, an exorbitant price, for 400 silver shekels for the field at Hebron (Genesis 23:16) is expensive, but 600 shekels of gold for the threshing floor is astronomical; in 2 Samuel 24:24, David pays only

50 shekels of silver. Only for the temple of God could this be considered a fair price!

The threshing floor thus purchased is the flat area on which the temple built by Herod the Great now stands; it is now known by Jews as the Temple Mount; by Muslims as the Dome of the Rock. It is north of and higher than the old City of David, for a threshing floor is always on a hill, since it catches the wind, which helps to separate the chaff from the grain.

5 David commissions Solomon to build the temple

1 Chronicles 28:1–10

The solemnity of this commission cannot be exaggerated. The list of officials at the beginning is matched by the description of the gathering as 'all Israel and the assembly of the Lord' (v. 8), a truly sacred and representative assembly. The solemnity is increased by the formal opening, 'King David rose to his feet and said...' (v. 2). David stresses the choice of himself as God's representative by a rehearsal of the gradually narrowing choice in verse 4: Israel, Judah for leader, the family of Jesse, himself as youngest son and then his own choice of Solomon. This last does manipulate the facts a little! The first two chapters of 1 Kings make clear that in fact at the last minute, when King David was nearing death, there was a fierce struggle over the succession. Solomon eventually won, but this involved slaughtering his rival Adonijah and several members of the old guard who opposed Solomon. So to say that David designated him at this solemn assembly is somewhat of a foreshortening, reading back from how it actually turned out. Be that as it may, the literary convention of a great figure giving final instruction and warnings to his successors was already well established in Greek and biblical literature (Socrates; 1 Samuel 8; later, Jesus at the last supper; Paul at Miletus). The Chronicler is interested not in the political infighting, but in the final result, the authority which Solomon eventually won.

It is fascinating that, before David hands over the detailed plans for the building, staffing and financing of the temple, he gives a commission to Solomon couched in the terms and language of Deuteronomic theology: 'If you seek him, he will let you find him; once forsake him and he casts you off forever'. This fourfold schema of infidelity–punishment–repentance–rescue was the theological message of the book of Deuteronomy and of the history in the books of Samuel and Kings, but it has much less importance in Chronicles. At the end of the commission, David also repeats that Deuteronomic motto: 'Be strong, stand firm, be fearless and set to work' (28:20), which comes repeatedly in the Deuteronomic history. Thus, in looking back at the very moment of the commissioning of the temple, the Chronicler gives an implicit warning of future disasters which were to occur and eventually destroy the temple.

6   David's final prayer

1 Chronicles 29:10–19

This noble final prayer of David does not, of course, stem from David but is put into his mouth by the Chronicler. The first chapter of 1 Kings presents a very different picture of the aged king, sustained by his prim and pretty carer Abishag, but at the mercy of the factions warring to succeed him. This detracts no whit from its nobility. It is a humble prayer, fully conscious that humans are strangers on earth whose days pass like a shadow, and that all sovereignty belongs to the Lord, who knows and judges the human heart. It begins and is filled throughout with praise for the Lord, to whom belong all greatness, power, splendour and length of days. As such, it is a fitting conclusion to the first half of this celebration of the temple built by David to perpetuate the divine worship.

There are also other aspects to this liturgical farewell. Most striking is the massive list of donations to the treasury with which this chapter opens (29:1–5), to be followed by similarly generous gifts to the sanctuary by the heads of families and the officials of the tribes (29:6–9). The same quantities of the same materials were donated in Exodus 25 and 35 to Moses for the sanctuary in the desert. There is indeed a constant underlying theme in these chapters that the succession of Solomon to David mirrors that of Joshua to Moses, not least in the Deuteronomic warning of future infidelity discussed in our previous section. To what extent is this generosity intended to be persuasive to those for whom the book was written? The temple would have been expensive not only to build and equip but also to maintain. The community of the returned exiles would not have been rich, and considerable generosity would have been required to maintain the very large personnel and the wealth of sacrificial offerings.

This issue raises the large question about the relationship of the book to an historical context after the return from exile. The books of Ezra and Nehemiah present a menaced community working to rebuild walls and temple with a builder's trowel in one hand and a sword in the other, not only threatened by the 'people of the land' (probably the descendants of remnants of the population who were not taken into exile) but viewed with suspicion by the local Persian overlords. The prophet Haggai similarly paints a picture of a discouraged population, none too willing to work wholeheartedly at the rebuilding. Even Isaiah 66:1–3, written well after the return from exile, questions the importance of the temple for true worship of the Lord. The book of Chronicles breathes a very different atmosphere.

Guidelines

It is possible to dismiss 1 Chronicles as a gathering of dry lists of genealogies and functionaries connected with the temple. That this would be a mistake is shown primarily by the atmosphere of joy, prayer and devotion which surfaces so frequently. Joy and rejoicing are keynotes of the ceremony of bringing the ark up to the City of David (15:16, 25). Gratitude and thanksgiving are keynotes of David's prayer after Nathan's promise (17:16–27). The arrival of the ark in Jerusalem is greeted with a song of praise, joy and devotion (16:8–36). The leaders are to devote themselves 'heart and soul to the search for the Lord' (22:19). Solomon is to serve God with an undivided heart (28:9). Joy is mentioned 21 times in this book, and heartfelt joy is the tone of all the prayers. David's final prayer (29:10–19) has a nobility all its own. The priests and Levites are preparing for no empty or formalistic liturgy, but for a heartfelt and devoted service of their God.

Romans: two at a time

Conrad Gempf

I have a friend with a lovely voice and a terrible habit: she sings out loud when she's wearing headphones. She's a genius at improvising harmony. But to the untrained ear (mine), hearing the harmony and not the melody, it sounds like she's murdering the song. You really want the two together.

A musical naïf like me wants the melody. Harmony, I tend to think, is an optional extra. But it isn't always. In some compositions, there are two lines and the whole point is hearing them together.

Similarly, the first time I heard the 'Farandole' from Bizet's *L'Arlésienne Suite No. 2*, I laughed out loud with delight. There are two motifs. The first is stately, almost pompous, and the piece starts by playing it twice. This is followed by a playful and frolicking flute and piccolo tune rushing around like a puppy, spraying violin splashes in every direction. There is then a section where the two themes vie for attention, interrupting each other. But in the finale, they are reconciled and are, incredibly, both played at once, fitting into each other in a way unimaginable from hearing them separately.

And that is what this two-week series is about. We will look at most of the chapters of Romans in pairs, allowing them to complement each other and bring out each other's depths and flavours. When we get to chapters 9—11, it makes sense to look at all three together.

Romans is the richest and fullest of Paul's letters. His thought is not a long list of individual topics. It is a closely woven, interconnected symphony. We will be focusing on the connections.

Unless otherwise stated, Bible quotations are from the New International Version (Anglicised).

1 How to react to sin

Romans 1 is a text about right and wrong. Natural revelation, the chapter says, is enough to point people to God. Humanity's neglect of him has led us into the practice of all sorts of wrong things (1:23–27). But it's not just a hiccup, it's a virus. Bad thinking and practice can harden into a bad mindset, which in turn can harden into a bad identity. Sin is a degenerating disease that, left to itself, will eat away everything.

For Christians looking for guidance about ethical conundrums, Romans 1 is often appealed to, on questions raised by homosexuality in particular. It appears from verses 26–27 that Paul regards homosexual practice as outside of God's intentions, as something 'unnatural' to which God 'abandons' people who have disregarded him.

But before we go *too* far down this road of using chapter 1 to make decisions about other people and their actions, we must look at the beginning of chapter 2.

Paul's words stay on the same street but turn a corner here: 'At whatever point you judge another, you are condemning yourself, because you who pass judgement do the same things' (2:1) He repeats in verse 3, 'When you… pass judgement on them and yet do the same things, do you think you will escape God's judgement?'

Paul seems here to be writing to Jewish Christians who would have judged Gentiles on their sexual behaviour. It is unlikely that Paul expects his readers to be committing *identical* sins when he talks about 'the same things', but is more likely saying that his readers' sins are of the same class and lead to the same ends. Therefore, they should be careful how they judge – not because there is no right and wrong, but because they too – and we too – are guilty of things *just as* serious and deadly.

Thus, chapter 2 helps us to hear chapter 1 differently. As if it is a piece of music, somehow the clear theme of 'there is right and wrong that matter very much' can be – must be – merged with the very different theme of 'judge not, lest ye be judged'. This is not a compromise reached by averaging two tones, but a harmony reached by allowing both notes to be themselves at once.

2 Sin is really against God, not against law

Romans 2:12–16; 3:20–21, 27–28

The law of Moses is the focus of Romans 2. Paul's view is complex. To understand the chapter properly, you need to know two things: first, where Paul has come from, and second, where Romans is going.

Remember that Paul was a Pharisee of Pharisees (Acts 23:6) and was probably addressing the Jewish Christians in this section of the book. You and I may not think the Jewish law is all that important, so we can read this chapter and be tempted to think that Paul is helping us appreciate how important law is. But the original readers would have had a very high view of the law (2:17). For them, this chapter is surprisingly strong in downplaying the importance of it.

What Paul establishes is that law is not as fundamental as some of the Roman Christians might have thought. Their thinking may have gone like this: God made the law; acting against that law is what we call sin. If this is right, then sin could be understood as 'disobeying orders'.

Instead, sin is first of all going against God's person, not his law. He was creator and king of the universe from the beginning. Sin is not disobeying orders as much as it is violating the creator–creature relationship. Law is secondary – almost descriptive rather than prescriptive. You can sin and perish apart from the law (2:12). God created the law to describe the relationship between himself and us. If the goal of life were obeying orders, then Jews (as the ones who received explicit orders) would have an advantage. But if the goal of life is an internal attitude not just external obedience (2:28), if it has to do with acknowledging and pleasing the king of the universe, then everyone in the universe is in a similar position. Through the law, the Jewish people were not made righteous; instead, through the law, they became aware of the sins they and everyone else were committing.

We need chapter 3 – where Romans is going next – to complete that thought: 'But now apart from the law the righteousness of God has been made known, to which the Law and the Prophets testify' (3:21). That means that just as you never needed a law to sin against God, so it should not be a surprise that now, you don't need the law to be restored by God.

3 Jew-plus-Gentile is not new

Romans 3:21–26; 4:13–17

One of the biggest surprises when you read Acts is just how long it takes for the Christians to realise that it's okay to share the gospel with Gentiles. In Acts 10, Peter is actually criticised for it, and in chapter 11, he's summoned to justify himself before the church in Jerusalem. It is difficult for us to conceptualise just how Jewish the first Christians were. They didn't mean to start Christianity; they thought they were just going where God was taking Judaism next.

An awareness of this motif explains why Paul needs chapter 4 to convince his Jewish Christian readers of what sounds obvious to us in chapter 3. Like melody and harmony, they needed to read these two chapters together.

When I was young, I had to memorise 'For all have sinned and fall short of the glory of God' (3:23). That mini-sentence is actually part of a larger sentence, and the clauses surrounding it emphasise the point Paul is really making. This sinfulness and new salvation affect all, Jew and Gentile alike. Imagine how this would have been felt by Jews: 'At least we Jews *have* the law and *try* to keep it. Those Gentiles don't even read it, much less keep it.' No, says Paul, all are equally in trouble with God. (Though it appears contradictory, what he means in 4:15 is that righteousness/unrighteousness is not about 'obeying orders' – at the time of Abraham there was no law to obey.)

In chapter 3, the biggest question Paul anticipates in reply is 'By coming to this conclusion, am I nullifying the law and the whole of the old covenant?' (3:31).

First, he answers, 'Not at all!' (3:31). But how can the Old Testament be true, if the new people of God are made up of both Jews and Gentiles, without discrimination? Chapter 4 unpacks that answer.

Simple, says Paul. Judaism *should* be about relationship with God. And that started way before the law. The relationship with God that Judaism intended to protect started with our ancestor Abraham – the father of many nations (Romans 4:17; Genesis 17:5).

Even though we no longer have the same biases or the same questions as the first Christians did, we can stand amazed to discover that God, in his infinite wisdom, had planned and prepared this all along.

4 The promise of old Abraham through the presence of a new Adam

Romans 4:13–17; 5:15–19

Chapter 4, as we've seen, is about Abraham. Paul must have loved to use him as an example. It's easy to see why: hundreds of years before the giving of the law, Abraham was able to have a relationship with God that was based on faith.

But wait. How is that faith able to save the Romans (or us, for that matter) when we're riddled with sin? Paul quotes Genesis 15:6, 'it was credited to him as righteousness', but wants to apply that to us: 'The words "it was credited to him" were written not for him alone, but also for us, to whom God will credit righteousness' (4:23–24). But how can this be?

Just as Paul needed a chapter 4 to unpack chapter 3, so now he needs what is in chapter 5 to help us understand how chapter 4 could be. And again, he probably revelled in being able to show how this 'brand new thing' that God was doing was clearly foreshadowed in the Old Testament – in the time even before the giving of the law.

Jesus accomplishes what was promised in Abraham – that the people of God would be made up of many nations – by using the same sort of spiritual 'mechanics' as in the story of the fall of Adam. Romans 5:12–19 is full of 'just as' language, culminating in 'just as through the disobedience of the one man the many were made sinners, so also through the obedience of the one man the many will be made righteous' (5:19).

This is the way things worked, and it is not by chance. Paul brings in the word 'gift' here, intending not only to make clear our unworthiness to receive (another pithy memory verse: 'While we were still sinners, Christ died for us', 5:8), but also especially to emphasise the intentionality of God in giving it. Adam acted carelessly and it infected us all. But in Jesus, God acted deliberately, giving a gift that overflows to us all (5:16). We will expand on this theme of 'gift' tomorrow.

To Jewish Christians like Paul, what God was doing in their day seemed shockingly new. But Paul shows that it was ancient – rooted and prepared for deep within their own Judaism. The promise made to Abraham is realised through the same mechanics as the fall. Hallelujah!

5 Freedom equals slavery

Dietrich Bonhoeffer gave us the phrase 'cheap grace' – I wonder what Martin Luther or Paul himself would have made of it. I'm sure that James would have loved it. When he wrote 'faith without deeds is dead' (James 2:26), he probably meant that the kind of 'faith' that is not lived out is mere 'belief' and is ineffectual in every way. Cheap grace refers to the way some Christians assume that since God gave salvation as a gift, there are no strings attached and no need to respond.

Paul is often thought to have taught this cheap grace. You could get that impression if you read chapter 5 without also reading chapter 6. We did nothing to inherit what Adam 'gave' us through his act of disobedience; it takes effect on us automatically. If you only read chapter 5, you might think that the same should be true of the work of the new Adam.

Like the brass in an orchestra, chapter 6 roars back at chapter 5. Paul begins, 'What shall we say, then? Shall we go on sinning, so that grace may increase?' (6:1). And he repeats the fallacious question a few verses later: 'What then? Shall we sin because we are not under the law but under grace?' (6:15).

He answers in an unfamiliar and unexpected way. We might expect him to answer that now we are free – it is a gift from God. But here in Romans, it turns out that he thinks of both law and faith as being like slavery, but to very different masters. 'You have been set free from sin and have become slaves to righteousness' (6:18).

Christianity is thus not without obligation. John Barclay, in his recent masterpiece *Paul and the Gift* (Eerdmans, 2015), argues cogently that the one thing that 'gift' did not mean in Paul's day was 'no strings attached'. Gifts were all about formalising or establishing a relationship. Repayment *in kind* may not have been expected, but these relationships were not without obligations. Indeed, strings may have been the very point of the gift.

For Paul, this gift of freedom does not mean you're unemployed with nothing but leisure time. It means you have a new job under a better, more humane boss! You no longer need obey the old abusive master whose wages are death. Your new master loves you!

6 Released – by death

Paul continues using unpleasant images for the freedom he is writing about, perhaps precisely to avoid the accusation that he was preaching the sort of gospel that James was against. Being a Christian is not a stroll in the park; it is a new slavery, it is death. Both themes are intertwined in both chapters, though chapter 6 emphasises slavery and 7 emphasises death.

To the first Roman readers, slavery was not just an idea or a practice of long ago. Slavery was real and current. Everyone in the Roman church would have seen and interacted with slaves every day; some in the church were slaves themselves. Paul writes, 'I am using an example from everyday life' (6:19). Slaves changing hands from one master to another would be almost as familiar an image to them as changing careers might be for us.

So, too, ancient people probably had more experience of death than we have. Paul uses this image in a clever analogy: just as death undoes the life-long bond of the marriage covenant, so also dying to sin with Christ undoes the bond to sin (7:2–4).

Sometimes Paul is accused of being unrealistic – he advises 'rejoice in everything' and can be seen to write as though Jesus solved all our problems. But this is not the complete Paul – his letters contain much about the difficulties that Christians face. And I believe that chapter 7 contains some of his thinking on this. It starts with a realisation that will have shocked a Pharisee like Paul: 'I found that the very commandment that was intended to bring life actually brought death' (7:10). Romans 7:15–25 is a passage that divides opinions. I take it to be about life as a Christian.

It is a powerful and realistic picture that begins 'I do not understand what I do. For what I want to do I do not do, but what I hate I do' (7:15). We have died to sin and the law – we are slaves who have changed hands so that sin and the law are no longer our master. But, as it must have been in real life, should the old master tell us to do something, there is still a tug to obey – at least until we hear our new master's voice (7:15–25).

Guidelines

Romans 1:16–17 provides a wonderful summary of the book. God's salvation is for everyone who believes, both Jew and Gentile. That salvation came to us in the form of Jesus. He acts as the second Adam, from whom we receive God's gift of salvation.

How might our lives be changed by what we read in the first chapters of Romans? I hope there are three emphases that stick with you.

- First, that sin is not so much 'disobeying orders' as it is 'being unfaithful' to a relationship. Behaviour is important, but actions are the symptoms, not the illness. When you confess your sins to God, focus on the restoration of relationship with him as much as on 'trying to do better'.

- Second, that our salvation can be viewed at the same time as a liberation and as a new slavery. It is slavery to the best master. Jesus' yoke is easy (Matthew 11:30); he is a loving master who has been through everything we have. The way to avoid serving your old masters is not so much to struggle against them as it is to teach yourself to listen to your new master's voice. Pray not for liberation but for his yoke.

- And the third is just the basic truth of how important it is to read scripture with scripture, and allow one passage or chapter to inform your reading of the other. As you read scripture this week, pray that the Spirit who inspired these words would inspire you to hold them together.

Romans is as close as Paul ever got to writing a systematic theology. He is dealing with big ideas like the place of law, sin, death, resurrection and salvation in God's overall plan. But there are practical points as well in these first chapters, and more in the chapters to come.

1 How to groan like a Christian

Romans 7:15–25; 8:23–31

'What I want to do I do not do, but what I hate I do' (7:15). I mentioned last week that I take this controversial passage to refer to the believers' experience of life on this planet. Those who disagree argue that there are many reasons for thinking 7:15–24 describes the life of Jews (compare 7:1), who have received the law and are trying to be faithful, rather than the Christian life, which he will only get to in chapter 8. Academics tend to take it that way, while pastors and devotional readers tend to identify with chapter 7 and interpret it as being about Christians. How can we know which is right?

The answer I want to posit is, of course, that we read the two chapters together. No one denies that chapter 8 is discussing Christian experience. Indeed, it is one of the most beautiful descriptions of our trying to live as heirs of God, serving time while waiting for God's salvation to be revealed. In chapter 8, we learn how to groan in a positive way; we learn that, as frustrating as the universe is under the fall, we are not groaning alone. The whole of creation feels just as we feel, and even the Spirit of God intercedes with groans too deep for words. We're in this together, and only for a while.

This positive view can be seen as the other side of the same coin as chapter 7. The experience there is described as a solitary one – it is me wrestling with myself, and that feels so negative. Chapter 7 expresses what many of us feel on our bad days. Nothing works the way it should, even for Christians. But, remember, chapter 8 reminds us – it's not just you *or* me, but you *and* me, and the whole of creation and the Spirit. We're in this together. And if he is with us and for us, who and what could possibly stand for long against us?

Thanks be to God, who delivers us and will deliver us even while we're all groaning for all we're worth!

2 Rays of hope for Israel

Three chapters stand at the centre of Romans and demand to be dealt with together. It is impossible to overstate how important the fate of the people of Israel was for Paul. The Lord God has now given what Jews desired for centuries. But most are rejecting it, thus turning themselves into enemies of their God. Observing that rejection fills Paul with anguish. In the course of the three chapters, Paul argues that God has the right to show or withhold mercy as he wishes (9:18), but that the problem is the Jews' wrongheaded pursuit of righteousness (9:32), so that they created their own way and rejected God's (10:3).

From there, the argument changes remarkably. God does not answer rejection with rejection (11:1). Paul presents four rays of hope. First, he refers back to Israel's history when there was a remnant who remained faithful (11:5). Second, he points out that sometimes hard hearts have been hardened by God himself (11:8). Pondering God's intentions for that hardening, Paul comes up with his third, perhaps most important, ray of hope. It's linked to his self-understanding as the apostle to the Gentiles whose heart's desire is for the Jews. One of the things that Jews expected in the age to come was for even the Gentiles to recognise God and his way. In the widespread conversion of Gentiles to Jesus, that was coming to pass! Perhaps Jews will envy the way that the Christians are succeeding where Judaism did not. Mightn't this help them to see Jesus as God's way, to repent and be grafted back in (11:24)?

The fourth ray of hope fits the 'first shall be last and the last first' reversals that both Jesus and Paul seemed to love. Gentiles (who were disobedient) have been shown mercy, and now Jews have become disobedient in order that they too might receive mercy – *through* the mercy shown to Gentiles (11:30–32). The beauty of this thought sends Paul into worship, as all good theology should (11:33–36)!

Once again, we find two things that should not exist together, but seem to, like two incompatible musical themes which the composer has created to be played out together. Those who persist in unbelief will be cut off (11:22–23), yet 'all Israel will be saved' – which Paul acknowledges is a 'mystery' (11:25–26).

3 If they deserve respect, then respect

Romans 12:17–18; 13:4–7

A stand-out theme in chapters 12—13 concerns our attitude towards rulers and authorities. By the time Paul wrote the epistle to the Romans, Christians had been persecuted by authorities in Jerusalem and Paul himself had been imprisoned wrongly by Gentile authorities. Given the history of the first Christians, one might expect Paul to write, 'Pay no mind to earthly authorities, but do what you know to be right and pleasing to God.' What he actually writes is surprisingly submissive (13:1, 5) and seems to ignore the persecution. But perhaps it isn't really that simple. At first glance, the chapter break begins the section on the government. But Paul didn't put in chapter breaks as such. When you look at the grammar of this section, there is a good reason for seeing a change of gear at 12:14 instead of at 13:1. 'Bless those who persecute you' (12:14) would be a good way to introduce how we are to deal with the authorities. Paul was writing to the city where the emperor lived. Actually, precisely at this time, people might have been saying, 'The Emperor is dead. Long live the Emperor,' as Nero took over from Claudius (who persecuted Jews and Christians, expelling them from Rome). Could this be why Paul writes about rejoicing and mourning with others in the middle of a section about trying to live in harmony (12:15)?

If this is right, then 13:1–5 is the middle, not the start, of a section of how Christians should live in a culture hostile to them. And what comes before and after acknowledges the difficulties. Bringing up taxes in 13:6–7 is significant. We do not have many sayings of Jesus specifically about the Roman emperor. But one that we do have comes in a brilliant story about divine and human authority: Mark 12:13–17. Was the coin created in Caesar's image? Give it to Caesar. Are you created in God's image? Then give yourself as a living sacrifice to God. 'Give to everyone what you owe them' (13:7). And do this knowing that a time is coming when God will judge the nations (13:11). Reading chapters 12 and 13 together, and hearing the underlying Jesus tradition, helps us see that Romans is not as uncritical of authority as it first appears. Give them what they deserve.

4 According to truth or according to love

Romans 13:8–10; 14:19–22

In chapters 13 and 14, we find ourselves once again dealing with a melody and harmony. Paul reflects Jesus' teaching about the end times here: we are to live as if it is upon us (13:11). But both chapters are united in exhorting us to keep on going (13:13; 14:19) and to act out of love.

In 13:8, Paul writes that acting in love will fulfil the law. He then lists several commandments which one fulfils more or less automatically if one starts by loving your neighbour as yourself. He has argued something similar in Galatians 5:14–23, where he specifically talks about living out this love as keeping 'in step with the Spirit' (Galatians 5:25).

But there is a paradox. Chapter 13 says that we will keep these commandments not by trying to keep them but by living in love. In chapter 14, Paul goes a very different direction and takes other commands (such as food laws or holy days) and argues that a person can act either way, except they should do the most loving thing (14:20–21).

Paul is convinced about God's view on the dispute: 'nothing is unclean in itself' (14:14). But he does not advocate, as a first solution to the squabbles, educating everyone about what the right thing is. Instead, of these food matters he dangerously writes, 'So whatever you believe about these things keep between yourself and God' (14:22). Let it go.

What a striking example of what he has been arguing. Following God is clearly a matter of expressing a relationship based in faith and love, and not based in following regulations. Paul does not believe, of course, that the commandments in 13:9 – 'You shall not murder,' 'You shall not steal' – are a matter of indifference. But they are non-negotiable not because they are commandments but because fulfilling them is a matter of love and faith rather than cold, calculated obedience.

In Pharisaism, so often the point seemed to be extending the law to cover every particularity. Paul has come a very long way from his background. He sees now that an obedience to the rules, if it is not based in faith and love, is wrong. And in the details of food and days, not keeping to the rules, if for reasons of love, is good.

5 Different practices, one mind and voice

Romans 14:2–6; 15:5–7

In these two chapters, Paul writes about two different groups, the strong and the weak. Their dispute seems to have been centred on what people should eat (14:2) but also about there being days that are more holy than others (14:5). This is not the only letter in which this dispute appears. We find similar things going on in 1 Corinthians 8. We can probably identify the weak with the Jewish Christians and those Gentile Christians who came to faith through their interest in Judaism. It would not be surprising that they still followed kosher food laws and honoured the sabbath. The strong would be the Gentile Christians and those who recognise that all food is clean and all days are holy. Paul believes that this is the correct position. (Note, however, saying all food is clean is not the same as saying anything natural can be consumed; Paul and other ancients knew about natural poisons!)

Throughout this series, we have experienced how looking at one chapter in light of another chapter completes or even changes our understanding. This is a delightful example on a much larger scale. Do you remember that an important theme at the very beginning of the book concerned how Jews, with their knowledge of the law, should not use that knowledge to pass judgement on Gentiles? What we find in chapters 14—15 is the exact reciprocal exhortation. The Gentile Christians have knowledge of how the gospel frees us to worship in Spirit and truth. But Paul tells them they should not use *their* knowledge of freedom in Christ to pass judgement on those who are still living by rules about foods and days.

There were, of course, no Baptists, Presbyterians, Lutherans or Anglicans in the first century. But there were, clearly, informal denominations that differed in practices. Paul's advice to them in chapter 15 unpacks the practices he advocated in chapter 14. But it also speaks to us in our coping with denominations with different ideas about God's preferences in worship and practice. 'May the God who gives endurance and encouragement give you the same attitude of mind toward each other that Christ Jesus had… Accept one another, then, just as Christ accepted you, in order to bring praise to God' (15:5, 7).

6 Inclusion: claims and names

Romans 15:7–9; 16:1–10

One of Paul's great declarations is that 'there is neither Jew nor Gentile, neither slave nor free, nor is there male and female, for you are all one in Christ Jesus. If you belong to Christ, then you are Abraham's seed, and heirs according to the promise' (Galatians 3:28–29). In Romans 15 and 16, he is explicitly writing about Jews and Gentiles, but, by the end, implicitly teaching us about the inclusion of all peoples. How can we hope to read chapters 15 and 16 together, you might wonder, since the latter looks to be little more than a long list of names, like the genealogies of the Old Testament and the gospels?

Well, it turns out that chapter 16 is a way of testing whether Paul actually lived out what he wrote about. We can easily imagine a person like Paul preaching 'equality' as a theoretical truth, but then, when it comes down to sending greetings, his buddies turn out to all be free, Jewish males.

Names can give us clues about the person. In our day, most of the time, you know from a name whether the person referred to is male or female. You also can often make a pretty good guess as to their nationality; consider, for example, if I told you I knew a Steven, a Stefan, a Stephen and a Stefanos. These features hold true of first-century names as well.

When we look at chapter 16, we indeed find Jews and Gentiles. We know Priscilla and Aquila (16:3) are Jews from what's written about them elsewhere; then comes Epenetus (16:5), an obviously Greek name, therefore likely a Gentile; then Mary (16:6), likely to be Jewish; and so on through the list. Often, Paul mentions when people are Jews (16:7, 11, 21).

In terms of slave and free, we know that Priscilla and Aquila are, like Paul, free tradespeople working in the tent business. The names Ampliatus and especially Urbanus (16:8–9) are thought to be slaves' names, but we don't have to guess when Paul greets 'households' without greeting the household owner (16:10–11) – those are slaves.

And although there are more males than females in the greetings section, women are well represented and often commended as hard workers rather than as the gentler sex!

Read together, chapters 15 and 16 demonstrate a Paul who practises what he preaches.

Guidelines

A major theme of Romans has been to stress the theological truth that faith relationship is more important than works of obedience and the law. This thrust is especially evident in chapters 1—8. Even chapters 9—11, which address a real-world problem for Paul, are discussed in theological, even theoretical, terms. But in the last few chapters, 12—16, Paul's writing turns extremely practical. By the middle of chapter 12, you could be forgiven for thinking you were reading Proverbs instead of a Pauline letter (12:9–19)!

But the practical bent springs from what comes before it: the consideration of Judaism, mercy and the worship with which chapter 11 ends. 'I urge you… in view of God's mercy, to offer your bodies as a living sacrifice, holy and pleasing to God – this is your true and proper worship' (12:1). What a contrast to the animal sacrifice so common to Jews and Gentiles! And when Paul unpacks how to do this worship in the following chapters, it concerns having an internal attitude that is lived out among others, and how that is more important than the rules and regulations.

This is my prayer for you and for myself as we come to the end of studying Romans, two at a time:

> May our lives be based in that relationship with God through Jesus in the Spirit, so that our eating and drinking, our celebrating of special days and even our groaning in frustration in the current age can be seen as a mark of living out our deep relationship with him and our love for each other. Amen

---

FURTHER READING

John Barclay, *Paul and the Gift* (Eerdmans, 2015) – in my view the most important book on Paul so far this century, helping us to recover a first-century perspective on the central idea of grace/gift.

Peter Oakes, *Reading Romans in Pompeii* (SPCK, 2009) – as intriguing as crime fiction, Oakes invites us to use real data from Pompeii to imagine the lives of first-century people and how they might have understood Romans.

John Stott, *Romans (The Bible Speaks Today)* (IVP, 1994) – a wonderfully clear and helpful companion from the ultimate pastor/scholar.

Overleaf... Guidelines forthcoming issue | Author profile | Recommended reading | Order and subscription forms

Guidelines forthcoming issue

DAVID SPRIGGS

How quickly the years run by. It's time to be thinking about Christmas again! At least, it is as I share with you some of the 'goodies' we have in store for the next issue of *Guidelines*.

Steve Walton brings his stimulating explanation of Luke's gospel to a climax as he takes us through the resurrection stories and the consequences for the future of the disciples. One of the most famous stories in this section of Luke is the walk to Emmaus. This clearly indicates that Jesus saw his mission through the Old Testament and provides one reason why, as Christians, we need to pay close attention to it.

The Old Testament has always been at the heart of my own studies, so let me whet your appetite with four substantial contributions on the Hebrew scriptures. Pauline Hoggarth presents the first of her two-part series on Jeremiah. In many ways, we feel we can know the heart of Jeremiah better than any of the other prophets. We are given glimpses of his youthful call to become a prophet; we share his sufferings, both physical as he is ill-treated by the powers that be and spiritual-psychological as he shares in both the suffering of God and the suffering of his people. Here is a rich encounter with scripture than can speak to us at many levels. The second offering is from Ernest Lucas on Proverbs – again, this is the first of two parts and offers us very insightful human encounters. Ernest's route is to unpack some of the themes that are scattered throughout Proverbs, including friends and neighbours, family relationships, sex and power.

The third contribution, by Bill Goodman, provides us with notes on Ezekiel. Ezekiel is a close compatriot of Jeremiah, but in most ways he is such a contrast. His priestly background shapes his experiences and his testimony to his encounters with God. Sometimes his imagery and sometimes his behaviour are hard to relate to but, like Jeremiah, he is called not only to be a spokesperson for God to his people but also to experience the sufferings of God and his people too. Just because of the apparent strangeness, we need to pay careful attention to this book. The fourth is by Jenni Williams on Deuteronomy, a book which seems to reflect the issues of exile and restoration while being rooted in the earlier history of Israel entering the promised land.

Then come two short contributions which explore links between the Old and the New Testaments. Walter Moberly unpacks the theme of 'exaltation and abasement' as it occurs in the Magnificat and then reflects back on Old Testament passages and forward into the gospels. Andrew Rogers provides us with some interesting insights on significant hermeneutical issues by reflecting on Christ's interpretation of the Old Testament in the Emmaus story, Paul's use of Moses' face shining because he has been in God's presence and the need to read with 'humility' – thus linking back to Moberly's contribution.

Next year, Andy Angel will continue his investigation of Matthew's gospel. As a lead into this, in the September issue he will help us think about Matthew's contribution to our understanding of Advent. Andrew Francis explores some of the scriptural significance of sharing meals together – which itself is a helpful contribution to this Christmas season and may prompt us to creative ways of carrying out Christ's mission, especially at this time of year. Harriet Mowat's focus is on ageing and family relationships – something which is of vital concern to our society and especially our Christian communities. Finally, let me mention Steve Hollinghurst's stimulating week on mission in the parables of Jesus.

I'm sure you'll agree with me that there is so much to look forward to in the next issue. I can't wait for it.

Author profile: Steve Walton

I was sitting in the chapel for morning worship at a theological college on the day of a job interview. At home, my wife, Ali, had been suffering from severe depression for a couple of years, which had caused her to leave the job she loved as a church minister. She was improving very slowly, and it wasn't clear how long her recovery would take. During the service, the Old Testament reading included this: 'I will restore to you the years which the swarming locust has eaten' (Joel 2:25, RSV). I was astonished, for I had been puzzling over how God could bring anything good from the difficult situation we were in, and yet here was the prophet Joel telling the people of Israel that God would repay them for the ecological devastation which swarms of locusts had brought to their crops. If God could do that for them, then he could certainly restore Ali's health. That verse sustained me for the three or so years which followed, as Ali slowly recovered and was able to resume her role as a pastor. Incidentally, I got the job, and being there was part of Ali's being able to recover, through having opportunities to teach in the college – and that bore further fruit much later in her becoming a theological college lecturer herself, further evidence of God restoring 'the years which the swarming locust has eaten'.

Through the Bible, I hear the voice of God. My habit is to read the whole Bible through every year, and I'm regularly struck by fresh things as I read. Sometimes, it's a challenge that comes from scripture, which calls me to respond by turning from wrong attitudes, thinking and behaviour. Sometimes, it's an encouragement that the Lord stands with me and will do good – as in the example from Joel. Sometimes, it's a piece of wisdom that shows me a situation I'm dealing with in a new light, and that enables me to meet that situation better.

Through the Bible, too, I'm given words to use to speak with God. The Psalms, particularly, have been a rich source of ways for me to pray in different situations. Whatever I'm feeling or experiencing, the Bible gives me ways to engage with God and address God about them. If I'm rejoicing, there are songs of praise. If I'm suffering, there are laments. If I need to have my eyes lifted above a tough situation to see that God still reigns, there are hymns of praise, such as those in Revelation 4—5.

I would have an impoverished life without the Bible. Although I study scripture as my job, as a professional biblical scholar, the reasons I do so come from my faith and experience of God through the Bible.

An extract from *Engaging the Word*

Engaging the Word sets out what biblical literacy means and what it looks like in our contemporary culture, exploring the benefits of biblical literacy for those who follow Jesus and for Christian leaders as local theologians and preachers. It also presents a series of practical explorations of the role of the Bible, which help us to reach up to God, reach in to develop our own identity in Christ and reach out to others. This extract is from chapter 2, 'Biblical literacy'.

We need the Bible as much today as we have ever needed it. Our society is destroying itself. We deny how our greed has damaged the earth; how our love of riches denies life to others; how our lifestyle impacts our neighbours' poverty. We face growing pressures that could mean the end of life on earth: nuclear war, terrorism, migration, climate change, viruses and diseases. We seem to be creating the kind of devastation that makes the book of Revelation seem almost mundane in its horror.

In his letter to his youthful apprentice Timothy, Paul talks about the terrible last days when people will love themselves and money:

> *People will be lovers of themselves, lovers of money, boastful, proud, abusive, disobedient to their parents, ungrateful, unholy, without love, unforgiving, slanderous, without self-control, brutal, not lovers of the good, treacherous, rash, conceited, lovers of pleasure rather than lovers of God – having a form of godliness but denying its power. Have nothing to do with such people.*

2 TIMOTHY 3:2–9 (NIV)

The antidote to such depravity and destruction, says Paul, is the Bible – or, rather, a sense of all that life brings with the word of God at the centre of our lives. There is a kind of multi-levelled Christianity here, based around that sense of the Word of God as both the presence of Jesus, the living Word, who brings alive the Bible, the written word, through the presence of the Spirit. All point to the presence of the Father – Word, Jesus, Spirit – the living Word testifying to the presence of God who uses his word to speak creation into existence (Genesis 1), who breathes life into Adam (Genesis 2), who breathes the Spirit into dead bones in the wilderness (Ezekiel 37), who brings Jesus back to life (John 20), who breathes the Spirit into the life of the disciples at Pentecost (Acts 2), who fills the church with the life and gifts of that same Spirit (Ephesians 4).

'You know all about my teaching, my way of life, my purpose, faith, patience, love, endurance, persecution, sufferings,' says Paul to Timothy (2 Timothy 3:10–11). You know my life, says Paul, and what empowers it, its engine: the word of God, the living Word, the living presence of Jesus Christ ('Christ in you, the hope of glory', Colossians 1:27). And he points out to Timothy the importance of the written word, the holy scriptures (literally, 'the holy writings', 2 Timothy 3:15): God-breathed, useful for teaching, rebuking, correcting, training in holiness, for equipping a servant of God for every good work, and for opening your eyes ('making you wise') to see the salvation available through faith in Jesus.

Opening our eyes in the Emmaus way seems to be a circular process – embracing, soaking ourselves in and breathing in the scriptures so that our minds might be opened to the wisdom that they contain and which they offer to us in return. We open ourselves to the transformative power of the word only to find the word transforming us to see the Bible in new ways. The Emmaus disciples had to speak of what they knew about Jesus and his ministry, his death and potential resurrection, then their eyes were opened. Timothy has absorbed the scriptures since he was young and now is encouraged to continue to seek after the living word. Biblical literacy, or biblicism, starts a cyclical process of reflection and engagement and absorption which develops us into the ideal readers of scripture ourselves: opening our eyes, opening our lives to all that scripture and God have to offer to us.

Biblical literacy is a process that is not just about reading the Bible, but about our eyes opened, our discipleship renewed, our lives transformed.

To order a copy of this book, please use the order form on page 149 or visit brfonline.org.uk.

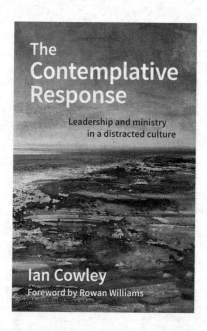

The true self finds peace in resting in the love of God, in the peace which Jesus promises. Jesus says to each of us in ministry, 'As the Father has loved me, so have I loved you. Abide, rest, dwell, in my love' (John 15:9). This book will seek to show what this might mean for those in Christian ministry in the 21st century.

The Contemplative Response
Leadership and ministry in a distracted culture
Ian Cowley
978 0 85746 656 3 £8.99
brfonline.org.uk

This book supplies principles and strategies for evangelism that are theologically rooted, practical and relevant to the 21st century. It shows how Jesus and the early church did evangelism and what we can learn from them for our situations. There is lots of practical help from two experienced practitioners to develop an evangelistic strategy for your church. It will also encourage leaders at every level of the church to be leaders and enablers in evangelism.

The Word's Out
Principles and strategies for effective evangelism today
David Male and Paul Weston
978 0 85746 169 8 £9.99
brfonline.org.uk

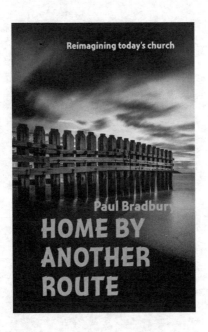

Reimagining today's church

Paul Bradbury

HOME BY
ANOTHER
ROUTE

Paul Bradbury believes that a movement of the Holy Spirit is beginning to renew and reform today's church – a church marginalised and 'in exile'. Following on from *Stepping into Grace*, Bradbury takes the prophet's powerful image of dry skeletal human remains coming to life through the miraculous work of the Spirit of God to encourage and inspire the contemporary church to seek renewal through the Spirit. This is a compelling and prophetic book – a must-read for today's church.

Home by Another Route
Reimagining today's church
Paul Bradbury
978 0 85746 631 0 £7.99
brfonline.org.uk

Tony Horsfall and Debbie Hawker encourage us to develop our resilience and to prepare ourselves for the challenges that life throws at us in an increasingly difficult world. Through biblical wisdom and psychological insight, they show us how to understand ourselves better, appreciate our areas of strength and strengthen our areas of weakness. Read this book if you want a faith that persists to the finishing line.

Resilience in Life and Faith
Finding your strength in God
Tony Horsfall and Debbie Hawker
978 0 85746 734 8 £9.99
brfonline.org.uk

To order

Online: brfonline.org.uk
Telephone: +44 (0)1865 319700
Mon–Fri 9.15–17.30

Delivery times within the UK are normally 15 working days. Prices are correct at the time of going to press but may change without prior notice.

Title	Price	Qty	Total
Engaging the Word	£7.99		
The Contemplative Response	£8.99		
The Word's Out	£9.99		
Home by Another Route	£7.99		
Resilience in Life and Faith	£9.99		
Eat, Pray, Tell	£7.99		
The Psalms	£9.99		

POSTAGE AND PACKING CHARGES			
Order value	UK	Europe	Rest of world
Under £7.00	£2.00	£5.00	£7.00
£7.00–£29.99	£3.00	£9.00	£15.00
£30.00 and over	FREE	£9.00 + 15% of order value	£15.00 + 20% of order value

Total value of books	
Postage and packing	
Total for this order	

Please complete in BLOCK CAPITALS

Title _____ First name/initials _____ Surname_____

Address_____

_____ Postcode _____

Acc. No. _____ Telephone _____

Email_____

Method of payment

☐ Cheque (made payable to BRF) ☐ MasterCard / Visa

Card no. ☐☐☐☐ ☐☐☐☐ ☐☐☐☐ ☐☐☐☐

Expires end [M][M] [Y][Y] Security code* ☐☐☐ Last 3 digits on the reverse of the card

Signature* _____ Date _____/_____/_____

*ESSENTIAL IN ORDER TO PROCESS YOUR ORDER

Please return this form to:

BRF, 15 The Chambers, Vineyard, Abingdon OX14 3FE | **enquiries@brf.org.uk**
To read our terms and find out about cancelling your order, please visit **brfonline.org.uk/terms**.

The Bible Reading Fellowship (BRF) is a Registered Charity (233280)

How to encourage Bible reading in your church

BRF has been helping individuals connect with the Bible for over 90 years. We want to support churches as they seek to encourage church members into regular Bible reading.

Order a Bible reading resources pack

This pack is designed to give your church the tools to publicise our Bible reading notes. It includes:

- Sample Bible reading notes for your congregation to try.
- Publicity resources, including a poster.
- A church magazine feature about Bible reading notes.

The pack is free, but we welcome a £5 donation to cover the cost of postage. If you require a pack to be sent outside the UK or require a specific number of sample Bible reading notes, please contact us for postage costs. More information about what the current pack contains is available on our website.

How to order and find out more

- Visit **biblereadingnotes.org.uk/for-churches**
- Telephone BRF on +44 (0)1865 319700 Mon–Fri 9.15–17.30
- Write to us at BRF, 15 The Chambers, Vineyard, Abingdon OX14 3FE

Keep informed about our latest initiatives

We are continuing to develop resources to help churches encourage people into regular Bible reading, wherever they are on their journey. Join our email list at **biblereadingnotes.org.uk/helpingchurches** to stay informed about the latest initiatives that your church could benefit from.

Introduce a friend to our notes

We can send information about our notes and current prices for you to pass on. Please contact us.

Transforming lives and communities

BRF is a charity that is passionate about making a difference through the Christian faith. We want to see lives and communities transformed through our creative programmes and resources for individuals, churches and schools. We are doing this by resourcing:

- **Christian growth and understanding of the Bible.** Through our Bible reading notes, books, digital resources, Quiet Days and other events, we're resourcing individuals, groups and leaders in churches for their own spiritual journey and for their ministry.
- **Church outreach in the local community.** BRF is the home of two programmes that churches are embracing to great effect as they seek to engage with their local communities: Messy Church and The Gift of Years.
- **Teaching Christianity in primary schools.** Our Barnabas in Schools team is working with primary-aged children and their teachers, enabling them to explore Christianity creatively and confidently within the school curriculum.
- **Children's and family ministry.** Through our Parenting for Faith programme, websites and published resources, we're working with churches and families, enabling children and adults alike to explore Christianity creatively and bring the Bible alive.

Do you share our vision?

Sales of our books and Bible reading notes cover the cost of producing them. However, our other programmes are funded primarily by donations, grants and legacies. If you share our vision, would you help us to transform even more lives and communities? Your prayers and financial support are vital for the work that we do. You could:

- support BRF's ministry with a regular donation (at **brf.org.uk/donate**);
- support us with a one-off gift (use the form on pages 153–54);
- consider leaving a gift to BRF in your will (see page 152);
- encourage your church to support BRF as part of your church's giving to home mission – perhaps focusing on a specific area of our ministry, or a particular member of our Barnabas in Schools team.
- most important of all, support BRF with your prayers.

Giving for the future

In 1942, as war raged across Europe and in the Pacific, William Beveridge published a radical report. In it, he argued for a state-run social security system that would fight the 'five giants' – want, disease, squalor, ignorance and idleness.

When World War II ended in 1945, the launch of the Welfare State was announced, and Beveridge's vision became a reality. Among other things, free education, social housing and a national health service (the NHS) providing care 'from the cradle to the grave' would soon be available to all.

The NHS has revolutionised Britain and its commitment to providing lifelong care means that many of us are living longer, healthier lives. Physical and emotional care are an important part of the picture, but they're not the only necessities for true well-being. Research has shown that attending to spiritual needs is just as important for our overall health.

At The Bible Reading Fellowship (BRF), we are passionate about helping people of all ages explore Christianity and grow in faith. Just like Beveridge, we want to provide care from the cradle to the grave. Whether you're a child of five attending Messy Church for the very first time or nearly 95 and enjoying the visits of an Anna Chaplain through BRF's The Gift of Years, we believe we have something that will help you take those important next steps on your spiritual journey.

If you share our vision for transforming lives of all ages through the Christian faith, would you consider leaving a gift in your will to BRF? We value every gift, small or large, and use them for significant projects with lasting impact.

For further information about making a gift to BRF in your will, please visit **brf.org.uk/lastingdifference**, contact Sophie Aldred on **+44 (0)1865 319700** or email **giving@brf.org.uk**.

Whatever you can do or give, we thank you for your support.

SHARING OUR VISION – MAKING A GIFT

I would like to make a gift to support BRF. Please use my gift for:

☐ where it is needed most ☐ Barnabas in Schools ☐ Parenting for Faith
☐ Messy Church ☐ The Gift of Years

Title	First name/initials	Surname

Address

	Postcode

Email

Telephone

Signature	Date

giftaid it You can add an extra 25p to every £1 you give.

Please treat as Gift Aid donations all qualifying gifts of money made

☐ today, ☐ in the past four years, ☐ and in the future.

I am a UK taxpayer and understand that if I pay less Income Tax and/or Capital Gains Tax in the current tax year than the amount of Gift Aid claimed on all my donations, it is my responsibility to pay any difference.

☐ My donation does not qualify for Gift Aid.

Please notify BRF if you want to cancel this Gift Aid declaration, change your name or home address, or no longer pay sufficient tax on your income and/or capital gains.

Please complete other side of form ➲

Please return this form to:
BRF, 15 The Chambers, Vineyard, Abingdon OX14 3FE

The Bible Reading Fellowship is a Registered Charity (233280)

SHARING OUR VISION – MAKING A GIFT

Regular giving

By Direct Debit: You can set up a Direct Debit quickly and easily at **brf.org.uk/donate**

By Standing Order: Please contact our Fundraising Administrator +44 (0)1235 462305 | **giving@brf.org.uk**

One-off donation

Please accept my gift of:

☐ £10 ☐ £50 ☐ £100 Other £ _____

by (*delete as appropriate*):

☐ Cheque/Charity Voucher payable to 'BRF'

☐ MasterCard/Visa/Debit card/Charity card

Name on card _____

Card no. ☐☐☐☐ ☐☐☐☐ ☐☐☐☐ ☐☐☐☐

Expires end ☐☐ ☐☐   Security code* ☐☐☐

*Last 3 digits on the reverse of the card
ESSENTIAL IN ORDER TO PROCESS YOUR PAYMENT

Signature _____ | Date _____

☐ I would like to leave a gift in my will to BRF.

For more information, visit **brf.org.uk/lastingdifference**

For help or advice regarding making a gift, please contact our Fundraising Administrator +44 (0)1235 462305

☛ Please complete other side of form

Please return this form to:
BRF, 15 The Chambers, Vineyard, Abingdon OX14 3FE

BRF

The Bible Reading Fellowship is a Registered Charity (233280)

GL0219

GUIDELINES SUBSCRIPTION RATES

Please note our new subscription rates, current until 30 April 2020:

Individual subscriptions
covering 3 issues for under 5 copies, payable in advance
(including postage & packing):

	UK	Europe	Rest of world
Guidelines 1-year subscription	£17.40	£25.50	£29.40
Guidelines 3-year subscription (9 issues)	£49.50	N/A	N/A

Group subscriptions
covering 3 issues for 5 copies or more, sent to one UK address (post free):

Guidelines 1-year subscription   £13.80 per set of 3 issues p.a.

Please note that the annual billing period for group subscriptions runs from 1 May to 30 April.

Overseas group subscription rates
Available on request. Please email **enquiries@brf.org.uk**.

Copies may also be obtained from Christian bookshops:

Guidelines   £4.60 per copy

All our Bible reading notes can be ordered online by visiting
biblereadingnotes.org.uk/subscriptions

For information about our other Bible reading notes,
and apps for iPhone and iPod touch, visit
biblereadingnotes.org.uk

GUIDELINES INDIVIDUAL SUBSCRIPTION FORM

All our Bible reading notes can be ordered online by visiting
biblereadingnotes.org.uk/subscriptions

☐ I would like to take out a subscription:

Title .... First name/initials .... Surname ....

Address ....

.... Postcode ....

Telephone .... Email ....

Please send *Guidelines* beginning with the September 2019 / January 2020 /
May 2020 issue (*delete as appropriate*):

(*please tick box*)

	UK	Europe	Rest of world
Guidelines 1-year subscription	☐ £17.40	☐ £25.50	☐ £29.40
Guidelines 3-year subscription	☐ £49.50	N/A	N/A

Total enclosed £ .... (cheques should be made payable to 'BRF')

Please charge my MasterCard / Visa ☐ Debit card ☐ with £ ....

Card no. ☐☐☐☐ ☐☐☐☐ ☐☐☐☐ ☐☐☐☐

Expires end ☐☐ ☐☐ Security code* ☐☐☐ Last 3 digits on the reverse
of the card

Signature* .... Date .... / .... / ....

*ESSENTIAL IN ORDER TO PROCESS YOUR PAYMENT

To set up a Direct Debit, please also complete the Direct Debit instruction
on page 159 and return it to BRF with this form.

Please return this form to:
BRF, 15 The Chambers, Vineyard, Abingdon OX14 3FE

To read our terms and find out about cancelling your order, please visit **brfonline.org.uk/terms**.

The Bible Reading Fellowship (BRF) is a Registered Charity (233280)

GL0219

GUIDELINES GIFT SUBSCRIPTION FORM

☐ I would like to give a gift subscription (please provide both names and addresses):

Title .... First name/initials .... Surname ....

Address ....

.... Postcode ....

Telephone .... Email ....

Gift subscription name ....

Gift subscription address ....

.... Postcode ....

Gift message (20 words max. or include your own gift card):

....

....

Please send *Guidelines* beginning with the September 2019 / January 2020 / May 2020 issue (*delete as appropriate*):

(*please tick box*)	UK	Europe	Rest of world
Guidelines 1-year subscription	☐ £17.40	☐ £25.50	☐ £29.40
Guidelines 3-year subscription	☐ £49.50	N/A	N/A

Total enclosed £ .... (cheques should be made payable to 'BRF')

Please charge my MasterCard / Visa ☐ Debit card ☐ with £ ....

Card no. ☐☐☐☐ ☐☐☐☐ ☐☐☐☐ ☐☐☐☐

Expires end ☐☐ ☐☐ Security code* ☐☐☐ Last 3 digits on the reverse of the card

Signature* .... Date ...... /...... /......

*ESSENTIAL IN ORDER TO PROCESS YOUR PAYMENT

To set up a Direct Debit, please also complete the Direct Debit instruction on page 159 and return it to BRF with this form.

Please return this form to:
BRF, 15 The Chambers, Vineyard, Abingdon OX14 3FE

To read our terms and find out about cancelling your order, please visit **brfonline.org.uk/terms**.

The Bible Reading Fellowship (BRF) is a Registered Charity (233280)

You can pay for your annual subscription to our Bible reading notes using Direct Debit. You need only give your bank details once, and the payment is made automatically every year until you cancel it. If you would like to pay by Direct Debit, please use the form opposite, entering your BRF account number under 'Reference number'.

You are fully covered by the Direct Debit Guarantee:

The Direct Debit Guarantee

- This Guarantee is offered by all banks and building societies that accept instructions to pay Direct Debits.
- If there are any changes to the amount, date or frequency of your Direct Debit, The Bible Reading Fellowship will notify you 10 working days in advance of your account being debited or as otherwise agreed. If you request The Bible Reading Fellowship to collect a payment, confirmation of the amount and date will be given to you at the time of the request.
- If an error is made in the payment of your Direct Debit, by The Bible Reading Fellowship or your bank or building society, you are entitled to a full and immediate refund of the amount paid from your bank or building society.
- If you receive a refund you are not entitled to, you must pay it back when The Bible Reading Fellowship asks you to.
- You can cancel a Direct Debit at any time by simply contacting your bank or building society. Written confirmation may be required. Please also notify us.

The Bible Reading Fellowship

Instruction to your bank or building society to pay by Direct Debit

Please fill in the whole form using a ballpoint pen and return it to:
BRF, 15 The Chambers, Vineyard, Abingdon OX14 3FE

Service User Number: | 5 | 5 | 8 | 2 | 2 | 9 |

Name and full postal address of your bank or building society

To: The Manager	Bank/Building Society
Address	
	Postcode

Name(s) of account holder(s)

Branch sort code

☐☐ - ☐☐ - ☐☐

Bank/Building Society account number

☐☐☐☐☐☐☐☐

Reference number

☐☐☐☐☐☐☐☐

Instruction to your Bank/Building Society
Please pay The Bible Reading Fellowship Direct Debits from the account detailed in this instruction, subject to the safeguards assured by the Direct Debit Guarantee. I understand that this instruction may remain with The Bible Reading Fellowship and, if so, details will be passed electronically to my bank/building society.

Signature(s)

Banks and Building Societies may not accept Direct Debit instructions for some types of account.

BRF

Transforming
lives and communities

Christian growth and understanding of the Bible

Resourcing individuals, groups and leaders in churches for their own spiritual journey and for their ministry

Church outreach in the local community

Offering two programmes that churches are embracing to great effect as they seek to engage with their local communities and transform lives

Teaching Christianity in primary schools

Working with children and teachers to explore Christianity creatively and confidently

Children's and family ministry

Working with churches and families to explore Christianity creatively and bring the Bible alive

parenting for faith

Visit **brf.org.uk** for more information on BRF's work

brf.org.uk